Jean Harries
Rec. July 1981
ST Davids

CW00819567

THE MONAD

THE MONAD

AND

OTHER ESSAYS UPON THE HIGHER CONSCIOUSNESS

BY

C. W. LEADBEATER

Fourth Reprint

1980

THE THEOSOPHICAL PUBLISHING HOUSE

ADYAR, MADRAS 600020, INDIA

68, Great Russell St., London WCIB 3BU, England

Post Box 270, Wheaton, Illinois 60187, U.S.A.

© The Theosophical Publishing House, Adyar, 1920

First Edition 1920
Second Printing 1947
Third Printing 1974
Fourth Printing 1980

ISBN   0-8356-0102-1

PRINTED IN INDIA

At the Vasanta Press, The Theosophical Society,
Adyar, Madras 600020

FOREWORD

THE essays included in this book are all upon subjects which it is of the highest importance that our students should try to understand. They have appeared during the last seven years in our various magazines. I have been asked to put them all together in a permanent form convenient for reference. Hence this volume.

C. W. L.

TABLE OF CONTENTS

CHAPTER I

THE MONAD

THE information available on the subject of the Monad is necessarily scanty. We are not at present in a position to supplement it to any great extent; but a statement of the case, as far as it is at present comprehended among us, may save students some misapprehensions, such as are often manifested in the questions sent in to us.

That many misconceptions should exist on such a subject is inevitable, because we are trying to understand with the physical brain what can by no possibility be expressed in terms intelligible to that brain. The Monad inhabits the second plane of our set of planes—that which used to be called the paranirvanic or the anupadaka. It is not easy to attach in the mind any definite meaning to the word plane or world at such an altitude as this, because any attempt even to symbolise the relation of planes or worlds to one another demands a stupendous effort of the imagination in a direction with which we are wholly unfamiliar.

Let us try to imagine what the consciousness of the Divine must be —the consciousness of the Solar Deity altogether outside any of the worlds or planes or levels which we ever conceived. We can only vaguely think of some sort of transcendent Consciousness for which space no longer exists, to which everything (at least in the Solar System) is simultaneously present, not only in its actual condition, but at every stage of its evolution from beginning to end. We must think of that Divine Consciousness as creating for Its use these worlds of various types of matter, and then voluntarily veiling Itself within that matter, and thereby greatly limiting Itself. By taking upon Itself a garment of the matter of even the highest of these worlds, It has clearly already imposed upon Itself a certain limitation; and, equally clearly, each additional garment assumed, as It involves Itself more and more deeply in matter, must increase the limitation.

One way of attempting to symbolise this is to try to think of it in connection with what we call dimensions of space. If we may suppose an infinite number of these dimensions, it may be suggested that each descent, from a higher level to a lower, removes the consciousness of one of these dimensions, until, when we reach the mental plane or world, the power of observing but five of them is all that is left to us. The descent to the astral level takes away one more, and the further descent to the physical leaves us with the three which are familiar to us. In order even to get an idea of what this loss of additional dimensions means, we have to suppose the existence of a creature whose senses are capable of comprehending only two dimensions. Then we must reason in what respect the consciousness of that creature would differ from ours, and thus try to image to ourselves what it would mean to lose a dimension from our consciousness. Such an exercise of the imagination will speedily convince us that the two-dimensional creature could never obtain any adequate conception of our life at all; he could be conscious of it only in sections, and his idea of even those sections must be entirely misleading. This enables us to see how inadequate must be *our* conception even of the plane or world next above us; and we at once perceive the hopelessness of expecting fully to understand the Monad, which is raised by many of these planes or worlds above the point from which we are trying to regard it.

It may help us if we recall to our minds the method in which the Deity originally built these planes. We speak with all reverence in regard to His method, realising fully that we can at most comprehend only the minutest fragment of His work, and that even that fragment is seen by us from below, while He looks upon it from above. Yet we are justified in saying that He sends forth from Himself a wave of power, of influence of some sort, which moulds the primeval pre-existent matter into certain forms to which we give the name of atoms.

Into that world or plane or level, so made, comes a second life-wave of divine energy; to it those atoms already existing are objective, outside of itself, and it builds them into forms which it inhabits. Meantime the first down-flowing wave comes yet again, sweeping through that newly-formed plane or level, and makes yet another, a lower plane, with atoms a little larger and matter therefore a little denser—even though its density may as yet be far rarer than our finest conception of matter. Then into that second world comes the second outflowing, and again in that finds matter which to it is objective, and builds of that its forms. And so this process is repeated and the matter grows denser and denser with each world, unitl at last we reach this physical level; but it will help us if we bear in mind that at each of these levels the ensouling life of the second outpouring finds matter already vivified by the first outpouring, which it regards as objective, of which it builds the forms which it inhabits.

This process of ensouling forms built out of already vivified matter is continued all through the mineral, vegetable and animal kingdoms, but when we come to the moment of individualisation which divides the highest animal manifestation from the lowest human, a curious change takes place; that which has hitherto been the ensouling life becomes itself in turn the ensouled, for it builds itself into a form (symbolised as the cup, the Holy Grail) into which the ego enters, of which he takes possession. He absorbs into himself all the experiences which the matter of his causal body has had, so that nothing whatever is lost, and he carries these on with him through the ages of his existence. He continues the process of forming bodies on lower planes out of material ensouled by the first outpouring from the Third Aspect of the Deity; but he finally reaches a level in evolution in which the causal body is the lowest that he needs, and when this is attained we have the spectacle of the ego, which represents the third outpouring from the First Aspect of the Deity, inhabiting a body composed of matter ensouled by the second outpouring.

At a far later stage the earlier happening repeats itself once more, and the ego, who has ensouled so many forms during the whole of a chain-period, becomes himself the vehicle, and is ensouled in his turn by the now fully active and awakened Monad. Yet here, as before, nothing whatever is lost from the economy of nature. All the manifold experiences of the ego, all the splendid qualities developed in him, all these pass into the Monad himself and find there a vastly fuller realisation than even the ego could have given them.

Of the condition of consciousness of the Solar Deity outside the planes of His system, we can form no true conception. He has been spoken of as the Divine Fire; and if for a moment we adopt that time-honoured symbolism, we may imagine that Sparks from that Fire fall into the matter of our planes—Sparks which are of the essence of that Fire, but are yet in appearance temporarily separated from it. The analogy cannot be pushed too far, because all sparks of which we know anything are thrown out from their parent fire and gradually fade and die; whereas these Sparks develop by slow evolution into Flames, and return to the Parent Fire. This development and this return are apparently the objects for which the Sparks come forth; and the process of the development is that which we are at the present moment concerned to try to understand.

It seems that the Spark, as such, cannot in its entirety veil itself beyond a certain extent; it cannot descend beyond what we call the second plane, and yet retain its unity. One difficulty with which we are confronted in trying to form any ideas upon this matter is that, as yet, none of us

who investigate are able to raise our consciousness
to this second plane; in the nomenclature recently
adopted we give to it the name of monadic because
it is the home of the Monad; but none of us have
yet been able to realise that Monad in his own
habitation, but only to see him when he has descended one stage to the plane or level or world
below his own, in which he shows himself as the
triple Spirit, which in our earlier books we call the
Ātmā in man. Even already he is incomprehensible,
for he has three aspects which are quite distinct and
apparently separate, and yet they are all funda-
mentally one and the same.

The Monad in his first aspect cannot (or at least
does not) descend below that spiritual level; but in
his second aspect he does descend into the matter of
the next lower world (the intuitional), and when
that aspect has drawn round itself the matter of that
level, we call it divine wisdom in man, or the
intuition. Meanwhile, the Monad in his third aspect
descends also to that intuitional plane and clothes
itself in its matter, and adopts a form to which as
yet no name has been attached in our literature.
It then moves forward or downward one more
stage, and clothes itself in the matter of the higher
mental world, and then we call it the intellect in
man. When that threefold manifestation on the
three levels has thus developed itself, and shows

itself as Spirit, intuition and intellect, we give to it
the name of the ego, and that ego takes upon himself a vehicle built of the matter of the higher
mental plane, to which we give the name of the
causal body. This ego, so functioning in his causal
body, has often been called the higher self, and
sometimes also the soul.

We see the ego then to be a manifestation of the
Monad on the higher mental plane; but we must
understand that he is infinitely far from being a
perfect manifestation. Each descent from plane to
plane means much more than a mere veiling of the
Spirit; it means also an actual diminution in the
amount of Spirit expressed. To use terms denoting
quantity in speaking of such matters is entirely
incorrect and misleading; yet if an attempt is to be
made to express these higher matters in human
words at all; these incongruities cannot be wholly
avoided; and the nearest that we can come, in the
physical brain, to a conception of what happens
when the Monad involves himself in matter of the
spiritual plane, is to say that only part of him can
possibly be shown there, and that even that part
must be shown in three separate aspects, instead
of in the glorious totality which he really *is* in his
own world. So when the second aspect of the
triple Spirit comes down a stage and manifests as
intuition, it is not the whole of that aspect which so

manifests, but only a fraction of it. So again when the third aspect descends two planes and manifests itself as intellect, it is only a fraction of a fraction of what the intellect-aspect of the Monad really is. Therefore the ego is not a veiled manifestation of the Monad, but a veiled representation of a minute portion of the Monad.

As above, so below. As the ego is to the Monad, so is the personality to the ego. So that, by the time we have reached the personality with which we have to deal in the physical world, the fractionisation has been carried so far that the part we are able to see bears no appreciable proportion to the reality of which it is nevertheless the only possible representation for us. Yet it is with and from this ridiculously inadequate fragment that we are endeavouring to comprehend the whole! Our difficulty in trying to understand the Monad is the same in kind, but much greater in degree, as that which we find when we try really to grasp the idea of the ego. In the earlier years of the Theosophical Society there were many discussions about the relations of the lower and the higher self. In those days we did not understand the doctrine even as well as we understand it now; we had not the grasp of it which longer study has given us. I am speaking of a group of students in Europe, who had behind them the Christian traditions, and the vague

ideas which Christianity attaches to the word
" soul "

The ordinary Christian by no means identifies
himself with his " soul," but regards it as something
attached to himself in some indefinite way—something for the saving of which he is responsible.
Perhaps no ordinary man among the devotees of
that religion attaches any very clear idea to the
word, but he would probably describe it as the im-
mortal part of him, though in ordinary language he
talks of it as a possession, as something separate
from him. In the *Magnificat*, the Blessed Virgin is
made to say: " My soul doth magnify the Lord, and
my spirit hath rejoiced in God my Saviour." She
may here be drawing a distinction between the soul
and the spirit, as St. Paul does; but she speaks of
them both as possessions, not as the I. She does
not say: " I as a soul magnify; I as a spirit
rejoice." This may be merely a question of language; yet surely this loose language expresses an
inaccurate and ill-defined idea. That theory was in
the air all about us in Europe, and no doubt we
were influenced by it, and at first to some extent
we substituted the term " higher self " for " soul ".

So we used such expressions as " looking up to
the higher self," listening to the promptings of the
higher self," and so on. I remember that Mr. Sin-
nett used sometimes to speak a little disparagingly

of the higher self, remarking that it ought to take more interest than it seemed to do in the unfortunate personality struggling on its behalf down here; and he used jokingly to suggest the formation of a society for the education of our higher selves. It was only gradually that we grew into the feeling that the higher self was *the man*, and that what we see down here is only a very small part of him. Only little by little did we learn that there is only one consciousness, and that the lower, though an imperfect representation of the higher, is in no way separate from it. We used to think of raising " ourselves " till we could unite " ourselves " with that glorified higher being, not realising that it was the higher that was the true self, and that to unite the higher to the lower really meant opening out the lower so that the higher might work in it and through it.

It takes time to become thoroughly permeated by Theosopical ideas. It is not merely reading the books, it is not merely hard study even, that makes us real Theosophist; we must allow time for the teaching to become part of ourselves. We may notice this constantly in the case of new members. People join us, people of keen intelligence, people of the deepest devotion, truly anxious to do the best they can for Theosophy, and to assimilate it as rapidly and perfectly as possible; and yet with all that, and with all their eager study of our books, they cannot at once put themselves into the position of the older members; and they will sometimes show that, by making some crude remark which is not at all in harmony with Theosophical teaching. I do not mean to suggest that the *mere* efflux of time will produce these effects, for obviously a man who does not study may remain a member for twenty years and be but little forwarder at the end of that time than he was at the beginning; but one who patiently studies, one who lives much with those who know, enters presently into the spirit of Theosophy—or perhaps it might be better said that the spirit of Theosophy enters into *him*.

Evidently, therefore, new members should never intermit their studies, but try to understand the doctrines from every point of view. Year by year we are all growing into the attitude of those who are older than ourselves, and it comes chiefly by association and conversation with those older students. The Masters know almost infinitely more than the highest of Their pupils, and so those highest pupils continue to learn from association with Them; we who are lower pupils know much less than those who stand above, and so we in turn learn by association with them; and in the same way those who are not yet even at our level may learn something from similar association with us. So always the older members can help the younger, and the younger have much to learn from those who have trodden the road before them. It was in this gradual way that we came to understand about the higher and the lower self.

It is a matter of exceeding difficulty to express the relation of the personality to the ego; as I have said above, I think that on the whole the best way to put it is to say that the former is a fragment of the latter, a tiny part of him expressing itself under serious difficulties. We meet a person on the physical plane; we speak to him; and we think and say that we know him. It would be a little nearer the truth to say that we know a thousandth part of him. Even when clairvoyance is developed—even when a man opens the sight of his causal body, and looks at the causal body of another man— even then, though he sees a manifestation of the ego on his own plane, he is still far from seeing the real man. I have tried, by means of the illustrations in *Man, Visible and Invisible*, to give some indication of one side of the aspect of these higher vehicles; but the illustrations are in reality absolutely inadequate; they can give only faint adumbrations of the real thing. When anyone of our readers develops the astral sight, he may reasonably say to us, as the Queen of Sheba said to King Solomon: " The half was not told me." He may say: " Here is all this glory and this beauty, which surrounds me in every direction and seems so entirely natural; it should be easy to give a better description of this." But when, having seen and experienced all this, he returns to his physical body and tries to describe it in physical words, I think he will find much the same difficulties as we have done.

For when, using the higher mental sight, a man ooks at the causal body of another, it is not actually the ego that he sees, but only matter of the higher mental plane which expresses the qualities of the ego. Those qualities affect the matter, cause it to undulate at different rates, and so produce colours, by examining which the character of the man can be distinguished. This character, at that level, means the good qualities which the man has developed; for no evil can express itself in matter so refined. In observing such a causal body, we know that it has within it, in germ, all the characteristics of the Deity—all possible good qualities, therefore; but not all of them are unfolded until the man reaches a very high level. When an evil feature shows itself in the personality, it must be taken to indicate that the opposite good quality is as yet undeveloped in the ego; it exists in him, as in every one, but it has not yet been called into activity. As soon as it *is* called into activity its intense vibrations act upon the lower vehicles, and it is impossible that the opposite evil can ever again find place in them.

Taking the ego for the moment as the real man, and looking at him on his own plane, we see him to be indeed a glorious being; the only way in which down here we can form a conception of what he really is, is to think of him as some splendid angel. But the expression of this beautiful being on the physical plane may fall far short of all this; indeed, it must do so—first, because it is only a tiny fragment; and secondly, because it is so hopelessly cramped by its conditions. Suppose a man put his finger into a hole in the wall, or into a small iron pipe, so that he could not even bend it; how much of himself, as a whole, could he express through that finger in that condition? Much like this is the fate of that fragment of the ego which is put down into this dense body. It is so small a fragment that it cannot represent the whole; it is so cramped and shut in that it cannot even express what it is. The image is clumsy, but it may give some sort of idea of the relation of the personality to the ego.

Let us suppose that the finger has a considerable amount of consciousness of its own, and that, being shut off from the body, it temporarily forgets that it is part of that body; then it forgets also the freedom of the wider life, and tries to adapt itself

to its hole, and to gild its sides and make it an enjoy-
able hole by acquiring money, property, fame and
so on—not realising that it only really begins to live
when it withdraws itself from the hole altogether,
and recognises itself as a part of the body. When
we draw overselves out of this particular hole at
night and live in our astral bodies, we are much less
limited and much nearer to our true selves, though
we still have two veils—our astral and mental bodies
—which prevent us from being fully ourselves, and
so fully expressing ourselves. Still, under those
conditions we are much freer, and it is much easier
to comprehend realities; for the physical body is
the most clogging and confining of all, and imposes
upon us the greatest limitations.

It would help us much if we could dissolve away
our limitations one by one; but it is not easy.
Realise how in the astral body we can move quickly
through space—not instantaneously, but still quickly;
for in two or three minutes we might move round
the world. But even then we cannot get anywhere
without passing through the intervening space. We
can come into touch at that level with other men
in their astral bodies. All their feelings lie open to
us, so that they cannot deceive us about them,
although they can do so with regard to their thoughts.
We see in that world many more of the earth's
inhabitants—those whom we call the dead—the

higher nature-spirits, the angels of desire, and many others. The sight of that plane enables us to see the inside of every object, and to look down into the interior of the earth; so that in many ways our consciousness is greatly widened.

Let us go a step further. If we learn to use the powers of the mental body, we do not therefore lose those of the lower, for they are included in the higher. We can then pass from place to place with the rapidity of thought; we can then see the thoughts of our fellow men, so that deception is no longer possible; we can see higher orders of the angels, and the vast host of those who, having finished their astral life, are inhabiting the heaven-world. Rising yet another step, and using the senses of the causal body, we find further glories awaiting our examination. If then we look at a fellow man, the body which we see within his ovoid is no longer a likeness of his present or his last physical body, as it is on the astral and mental planes. What we now see is the Augoeides, the glorified man, which is not an image of any one of his past physical vehicles, but contains within itself the essence of all that was best in each of them— a body which indicates more or less perfectly, as through experience it grows, what the Deity means that man shall be. By watching that vehicle we may see the stage of evolution which the man has reached; we may see what his past history has been, and to a considerable extent we can also observe the future that lies before him.

Students sometimes wonder why, if this be so, the evil qualitites which a man shows in one life should so often persist in later lives. The reason is not only that because the opposing good quality is undeveloped there is an opportunity for evil influences to act upon the man in that particular direction, but also that the man carries with him from life to life the permanent atoms of his lower vehicles, and these tend to reproduce the qualities shown in his previous incarnations. Then, it may be asked: " Why carry over those permanent atoms? " Because it is necessary for evolution; because the developed man must be master of *all* the planes. If it were conceivable that he could develop without those permanent atoms, he might possibly become a glorious archangel upon higher planes, but he would be absolutely useless in these lower worlds, for he would have cut off from himself the power of feeling and of thinking. So that we must not drop the permanent atoms, but purify them.

The task before most of us at present is that of realising the ego as the true man, so that we may let him work, instead of this false personal self with which we are so ready to identify ourselves. It is so easy for us to feel: " I am angry; I am jealous ";

when the truth is that that which is pushing us to anger or to jealousy is merely the desire-elemental, which yearns for strong and coarse undulations, which help him on his downward way into grosser matter. We must realise that the true man can never be so foolish as to wish for such vibrations as these —that he can never desire anything but that which will be good for his own evolution, and helpful for that of others. A man says that he feels impelled by passion. Let him wait and think: " Is it really I? " And he will discover that it is not he at all, but something else that is trying to get hold of him and make him feel thus. He has the right and the duty to assert his independence of that thing, and to proclaim himself as a free man, pursuing the road of evolution which God has marked out for him.

Thus it is at present our business to realise ourselves as the ego; but when that is fully accomplished, when the lower is nothing but a perfect instrument in the hands of the higher, it will become our duty to realise that even the ego is not the true man. For the ego has had a beginning—it came into existence at the moment of individualisation; and whatever has a beginning must have an end. Therefore even the ego, which has lasted since we left the animal kingdom, is also impermanent. Is there then nothing in us that endures, nothing that

will have no end? There is the Monad, the Divine
Spark, which is verily a fragement of God, an atom
of the Deity. Crude and inaccurate expressions,
assuredly; yet I know of no other way in which the
idea can be conveyed even as well as in words such
as these. For each Monad is literally a part of
God, apparently temporarily separated from Him,
while he is enclosed in the veils of matter, though
in truth never for one moment really separated.

He can never be apart from God, for the very
matter in which he veils himself is also a manifestation of the Divine. To us sometimes matter seems
evil, because it weighs us down, it clogs our faculties,
it seems to hold us back upon our road; yet remember that this is only because as yet we have not
learned to control it, because we have not realised
that it also is divine in its essence, because there is
nothing but God. A Sufi sage once told me that
this was his interpretation of the cry which rings
out daily in the call of the muezzin from the minaret
all over the Muhammadan world: " There is no God
but God, and Muhammad is the Prophet of God."
He told me that in his opinion the true mystical
meaning of the first part of this cry was: " There is
nothing but God." And that is eternally true; we
know that all comes from Him, and that to Him all
will one day return, but we find it hard to realise
that all is in Him even now, and that in Him it

eternally abides. All is God—even the desire-elemental, and the things which we think of as evil; for many waves of life come forth from Him, and not all of them are moving in the same direction.

We, being Monads, belonging to an earlier wave, are somewhat fuller expressions of Him, somewhat nearer to Him in our consciousness than the essence out of which is made the desire-elemental. In the course of our evolution there is always a danger that a man should identify himself with the point at which he is most fully conscious. Most men at present are more conscious in their feelings and passions than anywhere else, and of this the desire-elemental craftily takes advantage, and endeavours to induce the man to identify himself with those desires and emotions.

So when the man rises to a somewhat higher level, and his principal activity becomes mental, there is danger lest he should identify himself with the mind, and it is only by realising himself as the ego, and making *that* the strongest point of his consciousness, that he can fully merge the personality in the individuality. When he has done that, he has achieved the goal of his present efforts; but immediately he must begin his work over again at that higher level, and try gradually to realise the truth of the position we laid down at the beginning, that as the personality is to the ego, so is the ego to

the Monad. It is useless at our present stage to
endeavour to indicate the steps which he will have
to take in order to become a perfect expression of
the Monad, or the stages of consciousness through
which he will pass. Such conceptions as can be
formed of them may be arrived at by applying the
ancient rule that what is below is but a reflection of
that which exists in higher worlds, so that the steps
and the stages must to some extent be a repetition
upon a higher level of those which have already
been experienced in our lower efforts.

We may reverently presume (though here we are
going far beyond actual knowledge) that when we
have finally and fully realised that the Monad is the
true man, we shall find behind that again a yet further and more glorious extension; we shall find that
the Spark has never been separated from the Fire,
but that as the ego stands behind the personality,
as the Monad stands behind the ego, so a Planetary
Angel stands behind the Monad, and the Solar Deity
Himself stands behind the Planetary Angel. Perhaps, even further still, it may be that in some way
infinitely higher, and so at present utterly incomprehensible, a greater Deity stands behind the Solar
Deity, and behind even that, through many stages,
there must rest the Supreme over all. But here
even thought fails us, and silence is the only true
reverence.

For the time, at least, the Monad is our personal God, the God within us, that which produces us down here as a manifestation of him on these all but infinitely lower levels. What his consciousness is on his own plane we cannot pretend to say, nor can we fully understand it even when he has put upon himself the first veil, and become the triple Spirit. The only way to understand such things is to rise to their level, and to become one with them. When we do that we shall comprehend, but even then we shall be utterly unable to explain to anyone else what we know. It is at that stage, the stage of the triple Spirit, that we who investigate can first see the Monad, and he is then a triple light of blinding glory, yet possessing even at that stage certain qualities by which one Monad is somehow distinct from another.

Often a student asks: "But what have we to do with it while we are down here—this unknown glory so far above us?" It is a natural question, yet in reality it is the reverse of what should be; for the true man *is* the Monad, and we should rather say: "What can I, the Monad, do with my ego, and through it with my personality?" This would be the correct attitude, for this would express the actual facts; but we cannot truthfully take it, because we cannot realise this. Yet we can say to ourselves: "I know that I am that Monad, though as yet I cannot express it; I know that I am the ego, a mere fraction of that Monad, but still out of all proportion greater than what I know of myself in the personality down here. More and more I will try to realise myself as that higher and greater being; more and more I will try to make this lower presentation of myself worthy of its true destiny; more and more will I see to it that this lower self is ever ready to catch the slightest hint or whisper from above—to follow the suggestions from the ego which we call intuitions—to distinguish the Voice of the Silence and to obey it."

For the Voice of the Silence is not one thing always, but changes as we ourselves evolve; or perhaps it would be better to say that it *is* in truth one thing always, the voice of God, but it comes to us at different levels as we ourselves rise. To us now it is the voice of the ego, speaking to the personality; presently it will be the voice of the Monad, speaking to the ego; later still the voice of the Deity, speaking ·to the Monad. Probably, (as we have already suggested) between these last two stages there may be an intermediate one, in which the voice of one of the seven great Ministers of the Deity may speak to the Monad, and then in turn the Deity Himself may speak to His Minister; but always the Voice of the Silence is essentially divine.

It is well that we should learn to distinguish this voice—this voice which speaks from above and yet from within; for sometimes other voices speak, and their counsel is not always wise. A medium finds this, for if he has not trained himself to distinguish, he often thinks that every voice coming from the astral plane must necessarily be all but divine, and therefore to be followed unquestioningly. Therefore discrimination is necessary, as well as watchfulness and obedience.

Does the Monad, in the case of the ordinary man, ever do anything which affects or can affect his personality down here? I think we may say that such interference is most unusual. The ego is trying, on behalf of the Monad, to obtain perfect control of the personality and to use it as an instrument; and because that object is not yet fully achieved, the Monad may well feel that the time has not yet come for him to interfere from his own level, and to bring the whole of his force to bear, when that which is already in action is more than strong enough for the required purpose. But when the ego is already beginning to succeed in his effort to manage his lower vehicles, the real man in the background does sometimes intervene.

In the course of various investigations it has come in our way to examine some thousands of human beings; but we found traces of such intervention

3

only in a few. The most prominent instance is
that given in the twenty-ninth life of Alcyone, when
he pledged himself before the Lord Gautama to
devote himself in future lives to the attainment of
the Buddhahood in order to help humanity. That
seemed to us then a matter of such moment, and
also of such interest, that we took some trouble to
investigate it. This was a promise for the far-distant future, so that obviously the personality through
which it was given could by no means keep it;
and when we rose to examine the part borne in it
by the ego, we found that he himself, though full
of enthusiasm at the idea, was being impelled to
it by a mightier force from within, which he could
not have resisted, even had he wished to do so.
Following this clue still further, we found that the
impelling force came forth unmistakably from the
Monad. He had decided, and he registered his
decision; his will, working through the ego, will
clearly have no difficulty in bringing all future personalities into harmony.

We found some other examples of the same
phenomenon in the course of the investigations into
the beginnings of the Sixth Root Race. Looking
forward to the life in that Californian Colony, we
recognised instantly certain well-known egos; and
then arose the question: " Since men have free-
will, is it possible that we can already be absolutely

certain that all these people will be there as we foresee? Will none of them fall by the way?" Further examination showed us that the same thing was happening here as with Alcyone. Certain Monads had already responded to the call of the higher Authorities, and had decided that their representative personalities should assist in that glorious work; and because of that, nothing that these personalities might do during the intervening time could possibly interfere with the carrying out of that decision.

Yet let no one think, because this is so, that he is compelled from without to do this or that; the compelling force is the real you; none else than yourself can ever bind you at any stage of your growth. And when the Monad has decided, the thing will be done; it is well for the personality if he yields gracefully and readily, if he recognizes the voice from above, and co-operates gladly; for if he does not do this, he will lay up for himself much useless suffering. It is always the man himself who is doing this thing; and he, in the personality, has to realise that the ego is himself, and he has for the moment to take it for granted that the Monad is still more himself—the final and greatest expression of him.

Surely this view should be the greatest possible encouragement to the man working down here, this knowledge that he is a far grander and more glorious being in reality than he appears to be, and that there is a part of him—enormously the greater part —which has already achieved what he, as a personality, is trying to achieve; and that all that he has to do down here is to try to make himself a perfect channel for this higher and more real self; to do his work and to try to help others in order that he may be a factor, however microscopic, in forwarding the evolution of the world. For him who knows, there is no question of the saving of the soul; the true man behind needs no salvation; he needs only that the lower self should realise him and express him. He is himself already divine; and all that he needs is to be able to realise himself in al' the worlds and at all possible levels, so that in them all the Divine Power through him may work equally, and so God shall be all in all.

CHAPTER II

HIGHER CONSCIOUSNESS

STUDENTS who have not yet experienced the buddhic consciousness—consciousness in the intuitional world—frequently ask us to describe it. Efforts have been made in this direction, and many references to this consciousness and its characteristics are to be found scattered through our literature; yet the seeker after knowledge finds these unsatisfactory, and we cannot wonder at it.

The truth is that all description is necessarily and essentially defective; it is impossible in physical words to give more than the merest hint of what this higher consciousness is, for the physical brain is incapable of grasping the reality. Those who have read Mr. Hinton's remarkable books on the fourth dimension will remember how he tries to explain to us our own limitations with regard to higher dimensions, by picturing for us with much careful detail the position of an entity whose senses could work in two dimensions only. He proves that to such a being the simplest actions of our world must be incomprehensible. A creature who has no sense of what we call depth or thickness could never see any terrestrial object as it really is; he could observe only a section of it, and would therefore obtain absolutely wrong impressions about even the commonest objects of everyday life, while our powers of motion and of action would be utterly incomprehensible to him.

The difficulties which we encounter in trying to understand the phenomena even of the astral world are precisely similar to those which Mr. Hinton supposes to be experienced by his two-dimensional entity; but when we try to raise our thoughts to the intuitional world we have to face a state of existence which is lived in no less than six dimensions, if we are to continue at that level to employ the same nomenclature. So I fear we must admit from the outset that any attempt to comprehend this higher consciousness is foredoomed to failure; yet, as is but natural, the desire to try again and again to grasp something of it arises perennially in the mind of the student. I do not venture to think that I can say anything to satisfy this craving; the utmost that one can hope is to suggest a few new considerations, and perhaps to approach the subject from a somewhat different point of view.

The Monad in its own world is practically without limitations, at least as far as our solar system is concerned. But at every stage of its descent into matter it not only veils itself more and more deeply in illusion, but it actually loses its powers. If in the beginning of its evolution it may be supposed to be able to move and to see in an infinite number of these directions in space which we call dimensions, at each downward step it cuts off one of these, until for the consciousness of the physical brain only three of them are left. It will thus be seen that by this involution into matter we are cut off from the knowledge of all but a minute part of the worlds which surround us; and furthermore, even what is left to us is but imperfectly seen. Let us make an effort to realise what the higher consciousness may be by gradually supposing away some of our limitations; and although we are labouring under them even while we are thus supposing, the effort may possibly suggest to us some faint adumbration of the reality.

Let us begin with the physical world. The first thing that strikes us is that our consciousness, even of that world, is curiously imperfect. The student need feel no surprise at this, for he knows that we are at present only just beyond the middle of the fourth round, and that the perfection of consciousness of any plane will not be attained by normal humanity until the seventh round. The truth is that our whole life is imprisoned within limitations which we do not realise, only because we have always endured them, and because the ordinary man has no conception of a condition in which they do not exist. Let us take three examples; let us see how we are limited in our senses, our powers and our intellect respectively.

First, as to our senses. Let us take the sense of sight for an example, and see how remarkably imperfect it is. Our physical world consists of seven sub-planes or degrees of density of matter, but our sight enables us to perceive only two of these with anything approaching perfection. We can usually see solid matter, if it is not too finely subdivided; we can see a liquid that is not absolutely clear; but we cannot see gaseous matter at all under ordinary conditions, except in the rare instances in which it has an especially brilliant colour (as in the case of chlorine) or when it happens to be dense, to be much compressed, and to be moving in a particular way—as in the case of the air which may sometimes be seen rising from a heated road. Of the four etheric subdivisions of physical matter we remain absolutely unconscious so far as sight is concerned, although it is by means of the vibration of some of these ethers that what we call light is conveyed to the eye.

Let us then commence the imaginary process of removing our limitations by considering what would be the effect if we really possessed fully the sight of the physical world. I am not taking into consideration the possibility of any increase in the *power* of our sight, though no doubt that also will come in due course, so that we shall be able so to alter the focus of the eye as to make it practically a telescope or a microscope at will. I am thinking for the moment only of the additional objects that would come into our view if our sight were perfected.

Nothing would any longer be opaque to us, so that we could see through a wall almost as though it were not there, and could examine the contents of a closed room or of a locked box with the greatest ease. I do not mean that by etheric sight a man could see through a mountain, or look straight through the earth to the other side of it; but he could see a good way into the rock, and he could see down to a considerable depth in the earth, much as we can now see through many feet of water to the bottom of a clear pool.

One can readily see a score of ways in which the possession of such a faculty would be practically valuable, and it would manifestly add to our knowledge in many directions. All surgical work could be performed with an ease and certainty of which at present we have no conception, and there would be fewer cases of inaccurate diagnosis. We could see the etheric bodies of our friends, and so we should be able to indicate unfailingly the source and cause of any nervous affection. A whole fresh world would come under the observation of the chemist, for he would then be able to deal with ethers as he now deals with gases. Our sight would instantly inform us as to the healthiness or otherwise of our surroundings, just as even now our noses warn us of the presence of certain forms of putrefaction. We could see at once when we were in the presence of undesirable germs or impurities of any kind, and could take our precautions accordingly. We could study the great hosts of the fairies, of the gnomes and the water-spirits, as readily as now we can study natural history or entomology; the world would be far fuller and far more interesting with even this slight augmentation of our sense.

But remember that even this would not take us beyond the physical world; it would simply enable us to see that world more fully. We should still be liable to deception, we should still be capable of error with regard to the thoughts and feelings of others. We should still be blind to all the most beautiful parts of the life which surrounds us, even though we should see so much more of it than we do now. But even with the fullest physical sight we could see nothing as it really is, but only, at most, what corresponds to a looking-glass reflection of it. The two-dimensional entity could never see a cube; he would be quite incapable of imagining such a thing as a cube, and the nearest he could come to its comprehension would be to see a section of it as a square. However difficult it may be for us to grasp such an idea, we are at the present moment seeing only a section of everything that surrounds us; and because that is so, we think many things to be alike which are in reality quite different—just as to the two-dimensional creature the thinnest sheet of metal would appear precisely the same as a heavy block of it, the base of which had the same shape and area.

Then as to our powers. Here also we are strangely limited. However strong a man may be, however clever he may be at his speciality, whether that speciality be physical or mental, he can never work at it beyond a certain strictly limited extent without beginning to suffer from fatigue. Most people do not realize that this fatigue is always and entirely a physical disability. We speak of the mind as tired; but the mind cannot be tired; it is only the physical brain through which that mind has to express itself that is capable of fatigue. And even when the man is fresh and strong, how great are the difficulties in the way of a full expression of his thought! He has to try to put it into words; but words are feeble things at best, and can never really convey what the man feels or thinks; they are often misinterpreted, and the impression that they give is generally not at all what the speaker or writer originally intended.

The physical body is a serious obstacle in the way of rapid locomotion. Wherever we wish to go we have to carry with us this dense vehicle, this heavy lump of clay, that weighs the man down and checks his progress. At great expense and discomfort we must convey it by train or by steamer; and even with all our latest inventions, and with the wonderful progress that has been made with regard to all means of transportation, what a difficulty is this question of physical distance! How it stands in the way of the acquisition of knowledge; how it troubles the heart and lacerates the feelings of separated friends! The moment that we are able to raise our consciousness into a higher world all these difficulties are transcended.

Then as to our intellect. We are in the habit of boasting of it as some great thing. We speak of the march of intellect, of its great development, and generally speaking regard it as something of which we may reasonably be proud. Yet the truth is that it is nothing but a ridiculous fragment of what it presently will be—a fact which is abundantly clear to those of us who have had the privilege of coming into contact with some of the Masters of the

Wisdom, and seeing in Them what a fully developed intellect really is. Here again our studies ought to save us from the common error, for we know that it is the fifth round in each chain which is specially devoted to the development of the intellectual faculties; and as we are still in the fourth we naturally cannot expect that they should as yet be at all fully unfolded. In fact, at this stage they would be scarcely unfolded at all, if it were not for the stupendous stimulus that was given to the evolution of humanity by the descent of the Lords of the Flame from Venus in the middle of the Third Root Race.

All this is true; the physical consciousness is sadly limited; but how are we to transcend it? It might seem that in the ordinary process of evolution we ought to perfect the physical senses before we acquire those of the astral world; but our powers do not unfold themselves exactly in that way. In order that the man shall be able to function in his physical body at all, there must be an uninterrupted connection between the ego and that vehicle; and this involves the existence of the mental and astral bodies. At first they are employed chiefly as bridges across which communication passes; and it is only as our development progresses that they come into use as separate vehicles. But inevitably, while the consciousness is sending down messages through them, and receiving in return impressions through

them, they become to a certain small extent awakened; so that even in a savage, who cannot be said to
have any consciousness worth speaking of outside of
the physical vehicle, there is yet a faint dawning of
intellect and often a considerable amount of emotion.
At the stage where the ordinary man of civilised
countries stands at the present moment, his consciousness is on the whole more centred in his astral
body than in the physical, even though it is true
that the powers of the physical are as yet by no
means fully unfolded. Their stage of unfoldment
corresponds to the round in which we are now
engaged; at this period only a partial development
can be expected, but that partial development shows
itself to some extent in the mental and astral bodies,
as well as in the purely physical.

A good deal can be done even with the physical
body by careful training, but much more can be
done in proportion with the astral and mental
bodies, the reason being that they are built of finer
matter and so are much more readily amenable to
the action of thought. Even the physical body may
be greatly affected by that action, as is shown by
the remarkable performances of faith-healers and
Christian Scientists, and also by the well-authenti-
cated examples of the appearance of the stigmata
upon the bodies of some of those who have medi-
tated strongly upon the alleged crucifixon of the

Christ. But while only the few by determined exercise of thought-power can succeed in thus moulding the physical vehicle, anyone may learn how to control both the astral and the mental bodies by this power.

This is one of the objects which we seek to gain by the practice of meditation, which is the easiest and safest method of unfolding the higher consciousness. A man works steadily at his meditation year in and year out, and for a long time it seems to him that he is making no headway; yet all the while in his steady upward striving he is wearing the veil between the planes thinner and thinner, and at last one day there comes the moment when he breaks through and finds himself in another world. So wondrous, so transcendent, is that experience that he exclaims with startled delight:

" Now for the first time I really live; now at last I know what life means! I have thought before, that life on the physical plane could sometimes be fairly keen and brilliant—yes, even vivid and full of bliss; but now I realize that all that was the merest child's play—that even in my most exalted moments I had no comprehension, no faintest suspicion of the glorious reality."

And yet all this, which the man feels so intensely when for the first time he touches the astral world, will be repeated with still stronger force of contrast when he transcends that world in turn, and opens himself out to the influences of the mental level. Then again he will feel that this is his first glimpse of actuality, and that even the most wonderful incidents of his astral life were to this but " as moonlight unto sunlight and as water unto wine ". Again and again this happens to him as he climbs the ladder of evolution and comes nearer and nearer to reality; for verily it is true, as the old books have said, that " Brahman is bliss," and ever as one approaches the realization of Him that bliss increases.

But the higher the joy the greater the contrast between the inner life and the life of the physical world; so that to return from that to this seems like sinking into a profound abyss of darkness and despair. The contrast is indeed great; so great that one cannot wonder that many of the saints of old, having once tasted this higher bliss, forsook all in order to follow it, and retired to cave or to jungle that there they might devote themselves to this higher life, in comparison with which all else that men hold valuable seems but as dust before the wind. I remember that, in the early days of this Society, we were told in one of the letters which came through Madame Blavatsky, that when an adept had spent a long time in the nirvanic con- sciousness (leaving his body in a trance for weeks together), when he came back again into physical life he found the contrast so severe that he fell into a black depression which lasted for many days. Our terms were used very loosely in those days, and in this case the word adept must have referred to some one in the early stages of occult development —an adept merely in the sense that he was sufficiently accustomed to occult gymnastics to be able to leave his body and reside for a time upon a some-what higher level—not what we now mean by nirvana, for only a real Adept (in the sense in which we *now* use the word) could repose long upon the nirvanic level; and He is far too highly evolved and far too unselfish to allow Himself to indulge in depression, however intensely He may feel the change when He returns to this grey, dull earth from worlds of unimagined splendour. Neverthe-less the contrast is severe, and one who has found his true home in those higher worlds cannot but feel something of nostalgia while his duty compels him to dwell at the lower levels of ordinary life.

This has been spoken of as the great renunciation, and no doubt it is so; it would indeed be infinitely great, if one who has reached that point did not retain the powers of the higher consciousness even while still functioning in the physical body. One who has reached the Asekha stage, habitually carries His consciousness on the nirvanic level, even though

4

He still possesses a physical body. I do not mean that He can be fully conscious on both the planes simultaneously. When He is actually writing a letter or conducting a conversation on the physical plane, His consciousness is centred there, just like that of the ordinary man, though the spiritual splendour is still present in the background; but the moment that His physical work is over, the consciousness naturally springs back again to its accustomed condition, and though He still sits in the same physical chair, though He is fully alive and alert to all that is going on around Him, He is in reality living on that higher level, and earthly objects, though still present to Him, are slightly out of focus. This being His condition, the retaining of the physical body is only a modified sacrifice, although it involves a good deal of annoyance in the way of waste of time in eating, dressing, and so on.

When a man definitely attains the astral consciousness he finds himself much less hampered along all the three lines which we have instanced. In the astral body he has no longer sense-organs, but he does not need them, for what in that world corresponds to our senses works without needing a specialized organ. Strictly speaking, the word sight is hardly applicable to the perception of things in the astral world; but that knowledge of surrounding objects which we gain by seeing them is as readily and much more perfectly acquired in that higher vehicle. Every particle of the astral body is responsive, though only to vibrations of its own sublevel; thus in that higher life we get the effect of seeing all round us simultaneously, instead of only in one direction.

Since, as has frequently been explained, all solid physical objects have counterparts of that lowest type of astral matter which corresponds on that plane to a solid, we see practically the same world around us when utilising the astral senses. But it is a far more populous world, for now we are able to see the millions of the sylphs or air-spirits, and also the hosts of the dead who have not yet risen above the astral level. Higher beings also are now within our purview, for we can see that lowest order of the Angel evolution which we have frequently called the desire-angels. All our friends who still have physical bodies remain just as visible to us as before, although we see only their astral vehicles; but now all their emotions and passions lie open before us, and it is no longer possible for the conventionalist to deceive us as to the real state of his feelings on any point. His thoughts, however, are still veiled, except in so far as they affect his feelings, and so show themselves through them.

The limitation of space has not yet disappeared, but its inconveniences are reduced to a minimum.

We no longer need the clumsy methods of transportation with which we are familiar down here;
the finer matter of this higher world responds so
readily to the action of thought that merely to wish
to be at any place is at once to begin to journey
towards it. The journey still takes an appreciable
time, even though the amount is small and we can
reach the other side of the world in a few minutes.
But the few minutes are necessary, and we still
have the sensation of passing through space, and
can check ourselves at any moment of our journey,
so as to visit the intermediate countries.

The intellect is far freer here than in the lower
world, as it has no longer to exhaust most of its
strength in setting in motion the heavy and sluggish
particles of the physical brain. We gain greatly
also from the fact that fatigue has disappeared, so
that we are able to work steadily and continuously.
Another advantage is that we are far less hampered
at this level by pain and suffering. I do not mean
that there is no suffering in the astral world; on the
contrary, it may be in many ways more acute than
it can be down here, but on the other hand it can
much more readily be controlled. The astral world
is the very home of passion and emotion, and therefore those who yield themselves to an emotion can
experience it with a vigour and a keenness mercifully
unknown on earth. Just as we have said that most

of the strength of thought is spent in setting in motion the brain-particles, so most of the efficiency of any emotion is exhausted in transmission to the physical plane, so that all that we ever see down here is the remnant which is left of the real feeling, after all this work has been done by it. The whole of that force is available in its own world, and so it is possible there to feel a far more intense affection or devotion than we can ever gain amid the mists of earth. Naturally, the same thing is true with regard to the less pleasant emotions; accessions of hatred and envy, or waves of misery or fear, are a hundred times more formidable on that plane than on this. So that the man who has no self-control is liable to experience an intensity of suffering which is unimaginable amidst the benignantly-imposed restrictions of common life.

The advantage is that, little as most people realise it, in the astral world all pain and suffering is in reality voluntary and absolutely under control, and that is why life at that level is so much easier for the man who understands. No doubt the power of mind over matter is wonderful in all the worlds, and even down here it frequently produces marvellous and unexpected results. But it is exceedingly difficult to control by the mind acute physical pain. I know that it can often be done from outside by mesmerism, or even by determined exertion along the lines of Christian Science, and that it is frequently done in India and elsewhere by yogis who have made a speciality of it; but the power so to control severe pain is not yet in the hands of most people, and even where it is possible, such an effort absorbs so much of the energy of the man as to leave him capable of little else for the time but holding the pain at bay.

The reason of this difficulty lies in the density of the matter; it is so far removed in level from the controlling forces that their hold on it is by no means secure, and great practice is required before definite results can be produced. The far finer astral matter responds immediately to an exertion of the will, so that while only the few can perfectly and instantly banish severe physical pain, every one can in a moment drive away the suffering caused by a strong emotion. The man has only to exert his will, and the passion straightway disappears. This assertion will sound startling to many; but a little thought will show that no man *need* be angry or jealous or envious; no man *need* allow himself to feel depression or fear; all these emotions are invariably the result of ignorance, and any man who chooses to make the effort can forthwith put them to flight.

In the physical world fear may sometimes have a certain amount of excuse, for it is undoubtedly possible for one who is more powerful than we to injure our physical bodies. But on the astral plane no one can do hurt to another, except indeed by employing methods congruous to the plane, which are always gradual in their operation and easy to be avoided. In this world a sudden blow may actually injure the texture of the physical body; but in the astral world all vehicles are fluidic, and a blow, a cut, or a perforation can produce no effect whatever, since the vehicle would close up again immediately, precisely as does water when a sword has passed through it.

It is the world of passions and emotions, and only through his passions and emotions can man be injured. A man may be corrupted, and persuaded to harbour evil passions, unworthy emotions; but these after all can be induced only slowly, and any man who wishes to resist them can do so with perfect ease. Therefore there is no reason whatever for fear upon the astral plane, and where it exists it is only through ignorance—ignorance which can be dispelled by a few moments' instruction and a little practice. Also, most of the reasons which cause suffering amid terrestrial surroundings are quite unrepresented. When we lay aside this body, there is no longer hunger or thirst, cold or heat, fatigue or sickness, poverty or riches; what room is there then for pain and suffering? One sees at a glance that that less material world cannot but be a happier one for in that, far more than even in this, a man makes his own surroundings and can vary them at his will.

One of the greatest causes of suffering in our present life is what we are in the habit of calling our separation from those whom we love, when they leave their physical bodies behind them. Having only his physical consciousness, the un-instructed man supposes himself to have " lost " his departed friend; but this is really an illusion, for the departed friend stands beside him all the time, and watches the variations of feeling expressed in his astral body. It will at once be seen that it is impossible for the departed friend to be under any delusion that he has " lost " the loved ones who still retain physical vehicles, for since they must also possess astral bodies (or those physical vehicles could not live) the " dead " man has the living fully in sight all the time, though the consciousness of his living friend is available for the interchange of thought and sentiment only during the sleep of that friend's physical body. But at least the " dead " man has no sense of loneliness or separation, but has simply exchanged the day for the night as his time of companionship with those whom he loves who still belong to the lower world.

This most fertile source of sorrow is therefore entirely removed from one who possesses the astral consciousness. The man who has evolved to the point at which he is able to use fully both the astral and physical consciousness while still awake, can naturally never be separated from his departed friend, but has him present and fully available until the end of the latter's astral life, when that body in turn is dropped, and he enters upon his sojourn in the heaven-world. Then indeed an apparent separation does take place, though even then it can never be at all the same thing as what we call loss down here; for a man who has already fully realized the existence of two of the planes has thoroughly convinced himself of the plan of Nature's arrangements, and has a certainty with regard to them and a confidence in them which puts him in an altogether different position from the ignorance of the man who knows only one plane and cannot imagine anything beyond it.

In addition to this, a man who possesses astral consciousness has broken through the first and densest of the veils, and will find it no great effort to penetrate that which divides him from the mental world, so that it frequently happens that before the so-called " dead " person is ready to leave the astral plane, his friend has already opened the door of a yet higher consciousness, and is therefore able to accompany his " dead " associate in the next stage of his progress. Under any and all circumstances, and whether the man who is still in physical life is or is not conscious of what takes place, the apparent separation is never more than an illusion, for in the heaven-world the " dead " man makes for himself a thought-image of his friend, which is instantly observed and utilized by the ego of that friend; and in that way they are closer together than ever before.

Let us see what further advantages are gained by the man who has opened for himself the mental consciousness. Once again he passes through the experience already described, for he finds that this higher plane is thrilling with a glory and a bliss beside which even the wonderful vigour of the astral life pales its ineffectual fires. Once more he feels that now at last he has reached the true life, of which before he had only an inefficient and inaccurate reflection. Again his horizon is widened, for now the vast world of the Form-Angels opens before his astonished eyes. He sees now the whole of humanity—the enormous hosts who are out of incarnation as well as the comparatively few who possess vehicles upon the lower planes. Every man who is in physical or astral life must necessarily possess a mental body, and it is that which now represents him to the sight of the student who has come thus far on his way; but, in addition to this, the great army of those who are resting in the heaven-world is now within his view—though, as each is confined entirely within his own shell of thought, these men can hardly be regarded as in any sense of the word companions.

The visitor to their world can act upon them to the extent of flooding them with thoughts, say of affection. Sometimes these thoughts cannot so far penetrate the shell of the men who are enjoying their heaven-life as to carry with them any feeling of definite affection from the sender which could make them conscious of him, or evoke in them a reply directed personally towards him; but even then, the stream of affection can act upon the inhabitant of the heaven-world in precisely the same way as the warmth of the sun can operate upon the germ within the egg and hasten its fructification, or intensify whatever pleasurable sensations it may be supposed to have. Again, though these men in the heaven-world are not readily accessible to any influence from without, they are themselves pouring forth vibrations expressing the qualities most prominent in them; so the visitor to that world may bathe himself in such emanations as he chooses, and may go round selecting his type of emanation just as a visitor to Harrogate selects the variety of mineral water which he will drink, testing first one spring and then another.

Between those who are fully conscious on the mental plane there is a far closer union than has been possible at any lower level. A man can no longer deceive another with regard to what he thinks, for all mental operations lie open for every one to see. Opinions or impressions can now be exchanged not only with the quickness of thought, but with perfect accuracy, for each now receives the exact idea of the other—clean, clear-cut, instantaneous—instead of having to try to puzzle his way to it through a jungle of inexpressive words. At this level a man may circle the world actually with the speed of thought; he is at the other side of it even as he formulates the wish to be there, for in this case the response of matter to thought is immediate, and the will can control it far more readily than on any lower level.

It has often been said in connection with meditation that there is much greater difficulty in governing thoughts than emotions, and that the mental elemental is less susceptible to control than the astral. For us down here this is usually so, but if we wish to understand the matter aright, we must try to see why it is so. The physical body is along certain lines obedient to the action of the will, because we have carefully trained it to be so. If we desire to lift an arm, we can lift it; if we desire to walk to a certain place, if the physical body is in health, we can get up and walk to it with no more resistance on the part of the body than the expression of its ordinary indolence or love of ease. When, however, the physical body has set up bad habits of any kind, it often proves exceedingly refractory and difficult to restrain. It is in such cases that the distance and difference in density between the controlling ego and its lowest vehicle becomes painfully evident. The management of the astral vehicle is in reality much easier, though many people find it difficult because they have never previously attempted it. The moment that one really thinks clearly of the matter this is obvious. It is not easy to banish by thought-power a raging toothache, though even that can be done under certain conditions; it *is* comparatively easy by thought-power to banish depression or anger or jealousy. The desire-elemental may be persistent in obtruding these feelings upon the man's notice; but at any rate they clearly are under his control, and by repeatedly throwing them off, immunity from them can unquestionably be obtained.

Still more definitely is this true, and easier still ought to be our task, when we pass to the mental world. It seems to us more difficult to bridle thought than emotion, because most of us have made at least some experiments in the direction of repressing emotion, and we have been taught from childhood that it is unseemly to allow it to display itself unchecked. On the other hand we have been in the habit of allowing our thoughts to roam fancy-free, and it is probably only in connection with school lessons that we have reluctantly torn them back from their wanderings and tried to concentrate them on some definite task. To induce us to do even this much, exterior compulsion is usually required in the shape of constant exhortation from the teacher or the stimulus of emulation among our fellows in the class. It is because so little effort has been made by the average man in the direction of the regulation of thought that he finds it so difficult, and indeed almost impossible, when he begins the practice of meditation. He finds himself in conflict with the habits of the mental elemental, who has been used to have things all his own way, and to drift from subject to subject at his own sweet will.

Our struggle with him is in some ways different from that which we have already waged against the desire-elemental; and the reason for this will be obvious if we remember his constitution. He represents the downward-pouring life of the Solar Deity at the earliest stage of its immeshing in matter—that which we usually call the First Elemental Kingdom. Consequently, he is less used to material confinement than is the desire-elemental, who belongs to a later kingdom, and is one whole stage lower down in the scale of matter. He is

consequently more active than the desire-elemental
—more restless, but less powerful and determined;
he is in the nature of things easier to manage, but
much less used to management; so that it takes far
less actual exertion of strength to control a thought
than a desire, but it needs a more persistent appli-
cation of that strength. Remember that we are
now at the level of thought, where literally thoughts
are things; and this restive mental matter which
we find so difficult to govern is the very home
and definite vehicle of the mind with which we
are to control it. That mind is here on its own
ground and is dealing with its own matter, so that it
is only a question of practice for it to learn to
manage it perfectly; whereas, when we endeavour
to rule the desire elemental, we are bringing down
the mind into a world which is foreign to it, and im-
posing an alien ascendency from without, so that
we are badly equipped for the struggle.

To sum up then: control of mind is in itself far
easier than control of the emotions, but we have
had a certain amount of practice in the latter, and
as a rule almost no practice at all in the former;
and it is for that reason only that the mental exercise seems so difficult to us. Both of them together
constitute a far easier task than the perfect mastery
of the physical body; but this latter we have been
to some extent practising during a number of

previous lives, though our achievements along that line are even yet notably imperfect. A thorough comprehension of this matter should be distinctly encouraging to the student; and the result of such comprehension is vividly to impress upon him the truth of the remark made in *The Voice of the Silence* that this earth is the only true hell which is known to the Occultist.

Let us now take one step farther, and turn our attention to the upper part of the mental plane, which is inhabited by the ego in his causal body. Now at last the veils have fallen away, and for the first time we meet man to man without possibility of misunderstanding. Even in the astral world the consciousness is already so different from that which we know down here, that it is practically impossible to give any coherent idea of it, and this difficulty increases as we attempt to deal with higher planes. Here thoughts no longer take form and float about as they do at lower levels, but pass like lightning-flashes from one soul to another. Here we have no newly-acquired vehicles, gradually coming under control and learning by degrees more or less feebly to express the soul within; but we are face to face with one body older than the hills, an actual expression of the Divine Glory which ever rests behind it, and shines through it more and more in the gradual unfolding of its powers. Here we deal no longer with outer forms, but we see the things in themselves—the reality which lies behind the imperfect expression. Here cause and effect are one, clearly visible in their unity, like two sides of the same coin. Here we have left the concrete for the abstract; we have no longer the multiplicity of forms, but the idea which lies behind all those forms.

Here the *essence* of everything is available; we no longer study details; we no longer talk round a subject or endeavour to explain it; we take up the essence or the idea of the subject and move it as a whole, as one moves a piece when playing chess. This is a world of realities, where not only is deception impossible but also unthinkable; we deal no longer with any emotions, ideas or conceptions, but with the thing in itself. It is impossible to express in words the ordinary traffic of ideas between men in fully-developed causal bodies. What down here would be a system of philosophy needing many volumes to explain it, is there a single definite object—a thought which can be thrown down as one throws a card upon a table. An opera or an oratorio, which here would occupy a full orchestra for many hours in the rendering, is there a single mighty chord; the methods of a whole school of painting are condensed into one magnificent idea; and ideas such as these are the intellectual counters which are used by egos in their converse one with another.

There also we meet a higher order of Angels, more splendid but less comprehensible to our dull faculties. There for the first time we have fully unrolled before us all the stories of all the lives which have been lived upon our globe, the actual living records of the past; for this is the lowest plane on which the Divine Memory reflects itself. Here for the first time we see our lives as one vast whole, of which our descents into incarnation have been but the passing days. Here the great scheme of evolution is unfolded before us, so that we can see what is the Divine will for us.

The ordinary man is as yet but little developed as an ego; he needs the grosser matter of far lower planes in order to be able to sense vibrations and respond to them. But an ego who is awakened and is truly alive upon his own plane is indeed a glorious object, and gives us for the first time some idea of what God means man to be. The egos are still separate, yet intellectually they fully realize their inner unity, for they see one another as they are and can no longer blunder or fail to comprehend.

Strange as even that must seem when looked at from below, and far removed as it is from our ordinary conceptions of life, our next step brings us

into a region even less possible to be grasped by the
lower mind; for when we follow the man into the
intuitional world, developing the buddhic consciousness, we are in the presence not only of an indefinite extension of various capacities, but also of an
entire change of method. From the causal body we
looked out upon everything, understanding, seeing
everything exactly as it is and appraising it at its
true value, yet still maintaining a distinction
between subject and object, still conscious that we
looked upon that which we so thoroughly comprehended. But now a change has come; the comprehension is more perfect and not less, but it is from
within instead of from without. We no longer *look
upon* a person or upon an object, no matter with
what degree of kindliness or of sympathy; we simply *are* that person or that object, and we know him
or it as we know the thought of our own brain or
the movement of our own hand.

It is not easy even to suggest the subtle change
which this casts over everything—the curiously
different value which it gives to all the actions and
relations of life. It is not only that we understand
another man still more intimately; it is that we
feel ourselves to be acting through him, and we
appreciate his motives as our own motives, even
though we may perfectly understand that another
part of ourselves, possessing more knowledge or a

different view-point, might act quite differently.
All through our previous evolution we have had our
own private view-point and our own qualities,
which were cherished because they were our
own—which seemed to us in some subtle way
different from the same qualities when manifested
in others; but now we lose entirely that sense of
personal property in qualities and in ideas, because
we see that these things are truly common to all,
because they are part of the great reality which lies
equally behind all. So personal pride in individual
development becomes an utter impossibility, for we
see now that personal development is but as the
growth of one leaf among the thousands of leaves
upon a tree, and that the important fact is not the
size or shape of that particular leaf, but its relation
to the tree as a whole; for it is only of the tree as
a whole that we can really predicate permanent
growth.

Down here we meet people of different dispositions; we study them, and we say to ourselves
that under no conceivable circumstances could
we ever act or think as they do, and though we
sometimes talk of " putting ourselves in the other
man's place," it is generally a feeble, half-hearted,
insufficient substitution; but in the intuitional world
we see clearly and instantly the reason for those
actions which here seem so incomprehensible and

repugnant, and we readily understand that it is we ourselves in another form who are doing those very things which seem to us so reprehensible, and we recognize that to that facet of ourselves such action is quite right and natural. We find that we have ceased altogether to blame others for their differences from ourselves; we simply note them as other manifestations of our own activity, for now we see reasons which before were hidden from us. Even the evil man is clearly seen to be part of ourselves—a weak part; so our desire is not to blame him, but to help him by pouring strength into that weak part of ourselves, so that the whole body of humanity may be vigorous and healthy.

When in the causal body, we already recognized the Divine Consciousness in all; when we looked upon another ego, that consciousness leaped up in him to recognize the Divine within us. Now it no longer leaps to greet us from without, for it is already enshrined within our hearts. We *are* that consciousness and it is *our* consciousness. There is no longer the " you " and the " I ", for we both are one—both facets of something that transcends and yet includes us both.

Yet in all this strange advance there is no loss of the sense of individuality, even though there is an utter loss of the sense of separateness. That seems a paradox, yet it is obviously true. The man remembers all that lies behind him. He is himself, the same man who did this action or that in the far-off past. He is in no way changed, except that now he is much more than he was then, and feels that he includes within himself many other manifestations as well. If here and now a hundred of us could simultaneously raise our consciousness into the intuitional world, we should all be one consciousness, but to each man that would seem to be his own, absolutely unchanged except that now it included all the others as well.

To each it would seem that it was *he* who had absorbed or included all those others; so we are here manifestly in the presence of a kind of delusion, and a little further realization makes it clear to us that we are all facets of a greater consciousness, and that what we have hitherto thought to be *our* qualities, *our* intellect, *our* energy, have all the time been His qualities, His intellect, His energy. We have arrived at the realization in actual fact of the time-honoured formula: " Thou art that." It is one thing to talk about this down here and to grasp it, or think that we grasp it, intellectually; but it is quite another to enter into that marvellous world and *know* it with a certainty that can never again be shaken.

Yet it must not be supposed that when a man enters upon the lowest subdivision of that world, he at once becomes fully conscious of his unity with all that lives. That perfection of sense comes only as the result of much toil and trouble, when he has reached the highest subdivision of this realm of unity. To enter that plane at all is to experience an enormous extension of consciousness, to realize himself as one with many others; but before him then there opens a time of effort, a time of self-development, analogous at that level to what we do down here when by meditation we try to open our consciousness to the plane next above us. Step by step, sub-plane by sub-plane, the aspirant wins his way; for even at that level exertion is still necessary if progress is to be made.

A stage below this, while we were still in the higher mental plane, we learned to see things as they are, to get behind our preconceptions of them, and to reach the reality which lay behind what we had been able to see of them. Now we are able to see the reality which lay behind other people's divergent views of that same object; coming simultaneously up their lines as well as our own, we enter into that thing and we realize all its possibilities, because now it is ourselves, and its possibilities are possible also for us. Difficult to put into words; impossible fully to comprehend down here; and yet approaching and hinting at a truth which is more real than what we call reality in this world.

If we could instantly be transported to that level without passing slowly through the intermediate stages, most of what we found ourselves able to see would mean but little to us. The change abruptly even into the astral consciousness gives one so different an outlook that many familiar objects are entirely unrecognizable. Such a thing, for example, as a book or a water-bottle presents to us a certain appearance with which we are familiar; but if we suddenly find ourselves able to see that object from all sides at once, as well as from above and below, we shall perhaps realize that it presents an appearance so different that we should require a considerable amount of mental adjustment before we could name it with certainty. Add to that the further complication that the whole inside of the body is laid out before us as though every particle were separately placed upon a table, and we shall again see that additional difficulties are introduced. Add to them again yet another fact—that while we look upon all these particles as described, we are yet at the same time within each of those particles and are looking out through it, and we shall see that it becomes an absolute impossibility to trace any resemblance to the object which we knew in the physical world.

That is, of course, nothing but an illustration—a coarse and concrete example of what takes place;

and in order really to understand, one must spiritualize it and add to it many other considerations—all of which, however, tend to make the recognition more difficult rather than less. Fortunately in nature no sudden leap of this kind is possible. The method of evolution is gradual unfoldment, so that we are led on little by little until we are able to face without flinching glories which would dazzle us if they burst unexpectedly upon our view.

At this level man still has a definite body, and yet his consciousness seems equally present in vast numbers of other bodies. The web of life (which, you know, is constructed of buddhic matter—matter of the intuitional world) is extended so that it includes these other people, so that instead of many small separate webs we get one vast web which enfolds them all in one common life. But remember that many of these others may be entirely unconscious of this change, and to them their own private little part of the web will still seem as much separated as ever—or *would* do if they knew anything at all about the web of life. So from this standpoint and at this level it seems that all mankind are bound together thus by golden threads, and make one complex unit, no longer *a* man, but man in the abstract.

What can we say of the next stage of consciousness, that which has often been called nirvana?

This noble word has been translated to mean annihilation, but nothing could be further from the truth than this, for it represents the most intense and vivid life of which we know anything. Perhaps it may not unfairly be described as annihilation of all that we on the physical plane know and think of as the man; for all his personality, all his lower qualities, have long ago utterly disappeared. Yet the essence is there; the true man is there; the Divine Spark, descended from the Deity Himself, is still there, though now it has grown into a Flame—a Flame that is becoming consciously part of That from which it came; for here all consciousness merges into Him, even though it still retains all that was best in the feeling of individuality. The man still feels himself, just as he does now, but full of a delight, a vigour, a capacity, for which we have simply no words down here. He has in no way lost his personal memories. He is just as much himself as ever, only it is a wider self. He still knows that " I am I "; but he also realizes, and far more prominently, that " I am He ".

In the intuitional world his consciousness had widened so as to take in that of many other people. Now it seems to include the entire spiritual world, and the man feels that he is on the way to realizing the divine attribute of omnipresence; for he exists not only in all those others, but also at every point of the intervening space, so that he can focus himself wherever he will, thus realizing exactly the wellknown phrase that he is a circle whose centre is everywhere and its circumference nowhere. He has transcended intellect as we know it, yet he knows and understands far more fully than ever before. On lower planes (lower than this, yet to us high beyond all reaching) he has seen the great Angels and Archangels in all their glorious order. In this spiritual world he comes face to face with the powers that rule, with the great Administrators of Karma, with the great Leaders of the Occult Hierarchy, with Planetary Spirits of stupendous power and wondrous beauty.

It is hopeless to attempt to describe this life which transcends all life that we know, and yet is so utterly different from it as to seem almost a negation of it—a splendour of purposeful life as compared with a mere blind crawling along darkened ways. For this indeed is life and this is reality, as far as we can reach it at present; although we doubt not for a moment that beyond even this indescribable glory there extend yet greater glories which surpass it even as it surpasses this catacomb life of earth. There, all is God, and all these august Beings are obviously great manifestations of Him; and so thoroughly is this conviction borne in upon a man's consciousness, so entirely does it become part of him, that when he descends once more to the physical globe of this sorrowful star he cannot forget it, but ever thereafter he sees the Divine Spark, even in the most unlikely surroundings. Down here it is often hard to recognize; we need to dig so deeply in order to find it. In that spiritual world it is self-evident, and we know, because we see it, that there is nothing but God—no life anywhere in all the worlds but the Divine Life.

For at that level the man himself has become as a god among gods, a lesser light among the greater lights, yet truly an orb of splendour, even though so much less than the Masters, than the Great Devas, than the Mighty Spirits who rule the destinies of men and worlds. There we see face to face all these great Beings of whom down here we hear and read, of whom sometimes we make faint images. There we see with open face the beauty of which down here we can but catch the faintest reflections. There we hear the glorious music of the spheres, of which only occasional echoes can reach us in this lower world.

Truly terrible as is the descent from that great world to this, yet one who has once touched that consciousness can never again be the same as he was before. He cannot wholly forget, even amidst the darkness and the storm, that his eyes have seen the King in His beauty, that he has beheld the land which is very far off, and yet at the same time is near, even at our doors, close about us all the while, if we will but lift up our eyes to see it, if we will but develop the God within us till He can respond to the God without.

" The land which is very far off "; from the days of our childhood the phrase has been familiar to us, and it falls upon our ears with all the magic of holy associations; yet it is a mistranslation of the original Hebrew, and perhaps the real meaning of the text is even more beautiful and more appropriate, for the expression which Isaiah used is " the land of far distances," as though he were contrasting in his mind the splendid spaciousness of the star-strewn fields of heaven with the noisome narrowness of the cramped catacombs of earth. Yet even here and now, imprisoned in densest matter, we may lift our thoughts to the sun, for when once we know the truth, the truth has made us free. When once we have realized our unity with God, no darkness can ever shade us again, for we know that He is Light of Light, and the Father of Lights, with whom is no variableness, neither shadow of turning; and in Him is no darkness at all.

All this knowledge, all this glory, is within our reach, and must inevitably come to every one of us in the course of our evolution, as surely as day follows night. It is beyond all words now, beyond all feelings—beyond our intuition even. But there will come a time when we shall know even as now also we are known. All that will come to us in the course of nature (in the seventh round, as we have said), even though we drift along and make no exertion; but far earlier if we are willing to undertake the labour which earns it—hard work indeed, yet noble work and pleasant in the doing, even though at times it may bring with it much of suffering. Yet the way is the Way of Service, and each step that we take is taken not for ourselves but for others, that through our realization others may realize, that through our exertion others may find the Path, that through the blessing which comes to us the whole world may also be blessed.

CHAPTER III

THE BUDDHIC CONSCIOUSNESS

MUCH has been written about the buddhic or intuitional world, and all students are theoretically acquainted with its wonderful characteristic of unity of consciousness; but most of them probably regard the possibility of obtaining any personal experience of that consciousness as belonging to the far-distant future. The full development of the buddhic vehicle is for most of us still remote, for it belongs to the stage of the Fourth or Arhat Initiation; but it is perhaps not entirely impossible for those who are as yet far from that level to gain some touch of that higher type of consciousness in quite another way.

I was myself brought along what I should describe as the ordinary and commonplace line of occult development, and I had to fight my way laboriously upward, conquering one sub-plane after another, first in the astral world, then in the mental, and then in the buddhic; which means that I had the full use of my astral, mental and causal vehicles before anything came to me that I could define

certainly as a real buddhic experience. This method
is slow and toilsome, though I think it has its
advantages in developing accuracy in observation, in
making sure of each step before the next is taken.
I have no doubt whatever that it was the best for a
person of my temperament; indeed, it was probably
the only way possible for me; but it does not follow
that other people may not have quite other opportunities.

It has happened to me in the course of my work
to come into contact with a number of those who
are undergoing occult training; and perhaps the
fact which emerges most prominently from my experience in that direction is the marvellous variety
of method employed by our Masters. So closely
adapted is the training to the individual, that in no
two cases is it the same; not only has every Master
His own plan, but the same Master adopts a different scheme for each pupil, and so each person is
brought along exactly that line which is most suit-
able for him.

A remarkable instance of this variability of method
came under my notice not long ago, and I think that
an explanation of it may perhaps be useful to some
of our students. Let me first remind them of the
curious inverted way in which the ego is reflected
in the personality; the higher *manas* or intellect
images itself in the mental body, the intuition or

buddhi reflects itself in the astral body, and the spirit or *atma* itself somehow corresponds to the physical. These correspondences show themselves in the three methods of individualization, and they play their part in certain inner developments; but until lately it had not occurred to me that they could be turned to practical account at a much earlier stage by the aspirant for occult progress.

A certain student of deeply affectionate nature developed an intense love for the teacher who had been appointed by his Master to assist him in the preliminary training. He made it a daily practice to form a strong mental image of that teacher, and then pour out his love upon him with all his force, thereby flooding his own astral body with crimson, and temporarily increasing its size enormously. He used to call the process " enlarging his aura ". He showed such remarkable aptitude in this exercise, and it was so obviously beneficial to him, that an additional effort along the same line was suggested to him. He was recommended, while holding the image clearly before him, and sending out the love-force as strongly as ever, to try to raise his consciousness to a higher level and unify it with that of his teacher.

His first attempt to do this was amazingly successful. He described a sensation as of actually rising through space; he found what he supposed to

6

be the sky like a roof barring his way, but the force
of his will seemed to form a sort of cone in it,
which presently became a tube through which he
found himself rushing. He emerged into a region
of blinding light which was at the same time a sea
of bliss so overwhelming that he could find no words
to describe it. It was not in the least like anything
that he had ever felt before; it grasped him as
definitely and instantaneously as a giant hand might
have done, and permeated his whole nature in a
moment like a flood of electricity. It was more real
than any physical object that he had ever seen, and
yet at the same time so utterly spiritual. "It was
as though God had taken me into Himself, and I
felt His Life running through me," he said.

He gradually recovered himself and was able to
examine his condition; and as he did so he began to
realize that his consciousness was no longer limited
as it had hitherto been—that he was somehow
simultaneously present at every point of that marvellous sea of light; indeed, that in some inexpli-
cable way he *was* himself that sea, even though
apparently at the same time he was a point floating
in it. It seemed to us who heard, that he was
groping after words to express the consciousness
which, as Madame Blavatsky so well puts it, has
"its centre everywhere and its circumference
nowhere".

Further realization revealed to him that he had succeeded in his effort to become one with the consciousness of his teacher. He found himself thoroughly comprehending and sharing that teacher's feelings, and possessing a far wider and higher outlook on life than he had ever had before. One thing that impressed him immensely was the image of himself as seen through the teacher's eyes; it filled him with a sense of unworthiness, and yet of high resolve; as he whimsically put it.

"I found myself loving myself through my teacher's intense love for me, and I knew that I could and would make myself worthy of it."

He sensed also a depth of devotion and reverence which he had never before reached; he knew that in becoming one with his earthly teacher he had also entered the shrine of his true Master. with whom that teacher in turn was one, and he dimly felt himself in touch with a Consciousness of unrealizable splendour. But here his strength failed him; he seemed to slide down his tube again, and opened his eyes upon the physical plane.

Consulted as to this transcendent experience, I enquired minutely into it, and easily satisfied myself that it was unquestionably an entry into the buddhic world, not by toilsome progress through the various stages of the mental, but by a direct course along the ray of reflection from the highest astral sub-plane to the lowest of that intuitional world. I asked as to the physical effects, and found that there were absolutely none; the student was in radiant health. So I recommended that he should repeat the effort, and that he should with utmost reverence try to press higher still, and to raise himself, if it might be, into that other August Consciousness. For I saw that here was a case of that combination of golden love and iron will that is so rare on this our Sorrowful Star; and I knew that a love which is utterly unselfish and a will which recognizes no obstacles may carry their possessor to the very Feet of GOD Himself.

The student repeated his experiment, and again he succeeded beyond all hope or expectation. He was able to enter that wider Consciousness, and he pressed onward and upward into it, as though he were swimming out into some vast lake. Much of what he brought back with him he could not comprehend; shreds of ineffable glories, fragments of conceptions so vast and so gorgeous that no merely human mind can grasp them in their totality. But he gained a new idea of what love and devotion could be—an ideal after which to strive for the rest of his life.

Day after day he continued his efforts (we found that once a day was as often as it could be wisely attempted); further and further he penetrated into

that great lake of love, and yet found no end to it.
But gradually he became aware of something far
greater still; he somehow knew that this indescribable splendour was permeated by a subtler glory yet
more inconceivably splendid, and he tried to raise
himself into that. And when he succeeded he knew
by its characteristics that this was the Consciousness of the great World-Teacher Himself. In becoming one with his own earthly teacher he had
inevitably joined himself to the consciousness of
his Master, with whom that teacher was already
united; and in this further marvellous experience
he was but proving the close union which exists
between that Master and the Bodhisattva, Who in
turn had taught Him. Into that shoreless sea of
Love and Compassion he plunges daily in his meditation, with such upliftment and strengthening for
himself as may readily be imagined; but he can
never reach its limits, for no mortal man can fathom
such an ocean as that.

Striving ever to penetrate more and more deeply
into this wondrous new realm which had so suddenly
opened before him, he succeeded one day in reaching a yet further development—a bliss so much
more intense, a feeling so much more profound, that
it seemed to him at first as much higher than his
first buddhic touch as that had been above his
earlier astral experiences. He remarked:

" If I did not know that it is impossible for me
to attain it yet, I should say that this must be
Nirvana."

In reality it was only the next sub-plane of the
buddhic—the second from the bottom, and the sixth
from the top; but his impression is significant as
showing that not only does consciousness widen as
we rise, but the rate at which it widens increases
rapidly. Not only is progress accelerated, but the
rate of such acceleration grows by geometrical pro-
gression. Now this student reaches that higher
sub-plane daily and as a matter of course, and is
working vigorously and perseveringly in the hope
of advancing still farther. And the power, the
balance and the certainty which this introduces
into his daily physical life is amazing and beautiful
to see.

Another phenomenon which he observes, as
accompanying this, is that the intense bliss of that
higher plane now persists beyond the time of
meditation and is becoming more and more a part
of his whole life. At first this persistence was for
some twenty minutes after each meditation; then
it reached an hour; then two hours; and he is con-
fidently looking forward to a time when it will be
his as a permanent possession—a part of himself.
A remarkable feature of the case is that this prodigious daily exaltation is not followed by any sign

of the slightest reaction or depression, but instead produces an ever-augmenting radiance and sunniness.

Becoming gradually more accustomed to functioning in this higher and more glorious world, he began to look about him to some extent, and was presently able to identify himself with many other less exalted consciousnesses. He found these existing as points within his extended self, and he discovered that by focusing himself at any one of these points he could at once realize the highest qualities and spiritual aspirations of the person whom it represented. Seeking for a more detailed sympathy with some whom he knew and loved, he discerned that these points of consciousness were also, as he put it, holes through which he could pour himself down into their lower vehicles; and thus he came into touch with those parts of their lives and dispositions which could find no expression on the buddhic plane. This gave him a sympathy with the characters, a comprehension of their weaknesses, which was truly remarkable, and could probably have been attained in no other way—a most valuable quality for the work of a disciple in the future.

The wondrous unity of that intuitional world manifested itself to him in unsuspected examples. Holding in his hand one day what he regarded as a specially beautiful little object, part of which was white, he fell into a sort of ecstasy of admiration

of its graceful form and harmonious colouring.
Suddenly, through the object, as he gazed at it, he
saw unfolded before him a landscape, just as though
the object had become a tiny window, or perhaps a
crystal. The landscape is one that he knows and
loves well, but there was no obvious reason why the
little object should bring it thus before him. A curious
feature was that the white part of that object was
represented in the landscape by huge piles of cumulus
clouds, which he saw as floating in the sky of his
picture.

Impressed by this wholly unexpected phenomenon, he tried the experiment of raising his consciousness while he revelled in the beauty of the
prospect. He had the sensation of passing through
some resisting medium into a higher plane, and
found that the view before him had changed to one
which was strange to him, but even more beautiful
than that which he knew so well. The piles of
white cloud had become a towering snow-covered
mountain, with its long line sweeping down to a sea
of colour richer than any that in this incarnation
he had seen. The rocky bays, the buildings, the
vegetation, were all foreign to him, though well-
known to me; and by a little careful questioning I
soon ascertained without room for doubt that the
scene upon which he was looking was that which I
suspected—a real physical view, but one many

thousands of miles from the spot where he sat gazing at it. Since that hallowed spot is often in my mind, though I was not thinking of it at that moment, what the student saw may have been a thought-form of mine.

I imagine that up to this point what had happened may be quite simply described. I presume that the student's emotion was excited by his admiration, and that the heightened vibrations which were caused in this way brought into operation his astral senses, and this enabled him to see a view which was not physically visible, but well within astral reach. The endeavour to press on further temporarily opened the mental sense, and by it he was able to see my thought-form—if that second view was a thought-form of mine.

But the student did not rest satisfied with that; he repeated his attempt to push on still higher, or as he put it, still deeper into the real meaning of it all. Once more he had the experience of breaking through into some more exalted and more refined state of matter; and this time it was no earthly scene that rewarded his effort, for the foreground burgeoned forth into an illimitable universe filled with masses of splendid colour, pulsating with glorious life, and the snow-covered mountain became a great White Throne vaster than any mountain, veiled in dazzling golden light.

A strange fact connected with this vision is that the student to whom the experience came is entirely unacquainted with the Christian scripture, and was unaware that any text existing therein had any bearing upon what he saw. I asked him whether he could repeat this experience at will; he did not know, but later on he tried the experiment, and succeeded in passing again through those stages in the same order, giving some additional details of the foreign landscape which proved to me that this was not merely a feat of memory; and this time the awestricken seer whispered that amidst the coruscations of that light he once had a passing glimpse of the outline of a Mighty Figure Who sat upon the Throne. This also, you may say, might be a thought-form, built by some Christian of vivid imagination. Perhaps; but when a few days later an opportunity occurred, and I asked a Wise One what significa-tion we might attach to such a vision, He replied:

"Do you not see that, as there is but One Love, so there is but One Beauty? Whatever is beautiful, on any plane, is so because it is part of that Beauty, and if it is pushed back far enough, its connection will become manifest. All Beauty is of GOD, as all Love is of GOD; and through these His Qualities the pure in heart may always reach Him."

Our students would do well to weigh these words, and follow out the idea contained in them. All beauty, whether it be of form or of colour, whether it be in nature or in the human frame, in high achievements of art or in the humblest household utensil, is but an expression of the One Beauty; and therefore in even the lowliest thing that is beautiful all beauty is implicitly contained, and so through it all beauty may be realized, and He Who Himself is Beauty may be reached. To understand this fully needs the buddhic consciousness by which our student arrived at its realization; but even at much lower levels the idea may be useful and fruitful.

I fully admit that the student whose experiences I have been relating is exceptional—that he possesses a strength of will, a power of love, a purity of heart and an utter unselfishness which are, unfortunately, far from common. Nevertheless, what he has done with such marked success may surely be copied to some extent by others less gifted. He has unfolded his consciousness upon a plane which is not normally reached by aspirants; he is rapidly building for himself a capable and most valuable vehicle there—for that is the meaning of the ever-increasing persistence of the sense of bliss and power. That his is a definite line of progress, and not a mere isolated example, is shown by the fact that even already the abnormal buddhic development is producing its effect upon the apparently neglected causal and mental bodies, stimulating them into action from above instead of leaving them to be laboriously influenced from below as is usual. All this success is the result of steady effort along the line which I have described.

" Go thou and do likewise." No harm can come to any man from an earnest endeavour to increase his power of love, his power of devotion, and his power to appreciate beauty; and by such endeavour it is at least possible that he may attain a progress of which he has not dreamed. Only be it remembered that, in this path as in every other, growth is achieved only by him who desires it not for his own sake, but for the sake of service. Forgetfulness of self and an eager desire to help others are the most prominent characteristics of the student whose inner story I have here told; these characteristics *must* be equally prominent in any who aspire to follow his example; without them no such consummation is possible.

CHAPTER IV

AN INSTANCE OF PSYCHIC DEVELOPMENT

In the previous chapter I gave an instance of the abnormally rapid unfoldment of the buddhic faculty by means of the power of love; this case which I shall describe belongs to another line, for this time it is the faculty of the causal body which is aroused through the mental vehicle, by putting an undue strain upon the physical brain. But I cannot say to our readers in this case, as in the other: " Go thou and do likewise "; for the mental strain is a serious danger. It happened for once to lead to psychic development; but far more often it results in nervous breakdown of the gravest character, or even in brain lesion and insanity. The account sent to me is as follows:

" When I was at College (about 1910) I took up the study of the calculus, which, as you know, is the mathematics of variable quantities, the study of moving bodies and the like. From a variety of causes I was unable to do justice to the work day by day, and toward the end of the second term, when the day of examination in this was approaching, I was told by the lecturer that my work had been so unsatisfactory that unless I performed some miracle in the forthcoming examination he could not recommend me for a pass in the subject, I fully realized that he was quite right, and set about finding out how I could possibly score a high grade in the examination in order to offset the bad work during the year. I soon found that it would be impossible in the few days left to me really to understand the ground covered, and that the only hope would lie in memorizing the formulæ and applying them in a mechanical fashion to problems given in the examination. I therefore set to work, first to understand the definitions used in the text-books, and second to learn by rote all the important formulæ. I worked very hard, far into the night, neglected other subjects, in which I felt sure o' myself in any case, and resorted to all sorts of devices to gain time and keep awake. Bit by bit I covered all the important ground, but only by memorizing, sometimes even visualizing the *appearance* of a page or paragraph. The day of the examination I was utterly weary physically, but extraordinarily vivid mentally. I duly appeared, applied my crammed-up facts to the examination, and, as I subsequently found, wrote a paper with only one small mistake in arithmetical computation, or something like that. This was the unexpected performance that the lecturer demanded, and he duly gave me a pass.

"Now the point of this episode comes in the sequel. I found in a few days, as is usual in such cases, that all the material which I had stuffed into my head was a rapidly-vanishing jumble; but as it disappeared, and as I resumed my physical norm (chiefly by long hours of sleep), I discovered that I had actually done something, either damage or benefit, to my mental machinery, and that my ability to picture things in my mind was tremendously enlarged. I now found that if I turned my mind upon something I had seen or experienced even years before, the image returned to me, not in the ordinary vague way, but with the most extraordinary clarity in detail, with accompanying attributes of all sorts. For instance, if I was recalling a scene in a wood, I could actually *smell* the damp earth or the burning fire! This amused me very much, as it was quite possible to get back into the past in momentary flashes of the utmost brilliancy. After a time, however, the power of commanding this strange faculty wore off, and I had to be content with spontaneous outbursts which arose now and then through association. By the sight of a colour or some passing odour this latent power would suddenly put me into another time and place. Fortunately I could always banish the mental image, even though I could not call it up.

"After a time this gradually wore away into a lesser degree of brilliancy, and I was only occasionally edified by this annihilation of time and space.

"But now, just lately, there has been a return, in a new phase, of the old thing. I have had to learn, during the last year or so, the Government regulations of a business which I am carrying on. This had to be accomplished quickly, and I find that with this effort there is a return of the result which followed the previous effort, and, it is pleasant to note, with two new aspects; first that I am much more able to command and sustain any image that arises, and second that I can *magnify* the scene to a certain extent. Thus, if the picture includes a wall in the distance I can occasionally magnify it until the crannies are visible. And, what astonished me exceedingly, if there is a perfume, say, of flowers present, the same microscopic power can be turned on! Now the result is not intensification of the perfume, as one might hastily conclude, but a *roughening* of it. I mean by this that instead of getting thicker, in the sense that a heavy oil is thicker than water, the smell loses its smoothness and becomes (if one could feel it) like woollen cloth, or a basin of sand. For some reason I cannot perform this same enlarging trick with sound. At present there is no sign of any diminution of this curious phase of memory, but I have no doubt that it will fade away in large part, as I am too busy to undertake its cultivation."

What is happening in this case is obvious to any-one who has had experience in the use of the higher faculties. Instead of using his memory in the ordinary way, the student is coming into touch with the Records; and that means that he is to a certain extent employing the faculties of his causal body. We are far from certain as to the exact method of ordinary memory, for the subject has not yet been investigated; but it is clear that a vibration in the mental body is part of what occurs, and that the causal body is not in any way involved. In the reading of the Records it is precisely this latter sheath through which the work is done, and the mental body vibrates only in response to the activity of the causal. For that reason no satisfactory or reliable reading of the Records can be done without definite development of the vehicle of the ego.

From the description which our student gives, it is clear that he was using his causal body in the

7

glimpses of the past which he relates. It is also evident that that vehicle was aroused by the undue pressure put upon the mind by his reckless over-work. Most men would have ruined their health for life if they had pushed the strain as far as he did; he happens to be the one in a million who managed to do this thing and survive. The result is that his steady persistence in keeping up high mental undulations has stirred his causal body into activity, and thus endued him with a faculty different from any which he has before possessed.

So far it seems to waken only when he turns his thoughts to the past, and only in connection with scenes already familiar to him; but it is probable that he will soon find that he can extend its working in various ways. When a scene is clearly in mind it might be possible to move backwards or forwards from it, and so recover detailed memory of large sections of early life. Perhaps one could in this way push back recollection into childhood—back to birth itself, and even beyond; there have been those who in this manner have attained full knowledge of previous incarnations. Practice makes perfect; and it is encouraging that the power is much more under control now than formerly. The faculty of magnification is another conclusive proof that it is the causal body which is being used; this feature also might by degrees be largely increased, and when fully at the student's disposal might be used (for example) to undertake researches into occult chemistry.

The description of the " roughening " of the smell is most characteristic. The actual process of magnifying consists not in increasing the size of the object examined, but in lessening the psychic lens through which that object is seen. In ancient scriptures it is said that the operator makes himself as small as he will, and so the organ of vision which he is using becomes commensurate with the microscopic size of that at which he looks. Consequently the tiny physical particles which call into action the sense of smell become separately appreciable, like the grains upon sandpaper, and so the sense of roughness is·produced. It is a thing difficult to put into words, but anyone who has used the higher faculty will at once recognize our student's attempt to express it.

He is much to be congratulated upon his result, though we certainly cannot recommend his method for imitation by others. Such development will come easily and naturally when, in the course of human evolution, the mind has grown more nearly to the limit of its capabilities; but at our present stage such pressure is distinctly dangerous. That even this partial unfoldment should have been safely achieved is a sign of the times—a sign of the strength of the spiritual outpouring which even now is flooding the world.

CHAPTER V

TIME

THERE are two kinds of time: our time and God's time; two at least, but probably many more; for while we know something of our own capacity, we have no means of gauging the divine capacity. Our consciousness is a point, moving ever from the past to the future, and we give the name of "the present" to the passing moment which divides the two; but this "present" is an illusion; it is evanescent—a mere knife-edge. Even while we think of that moment, it has already become the past, and another moment is to us the present.

Our consciousness moves along a certain line—say, for the sake of illustration, from south to north. Our memory includes more or less accurately that part of the line over which we have already passed, but not that which still lies before us; and we usually regard what we call the past as irrevocable, whereas we recognize that we possess a certain amount of power to mould our future. That is because we think that the point which is our consciousness has already moved along a certain line which cannot now be altered; but that its future movements may to some extent be controlled, since to us it appears that the events of the future have not yet happened. It is true that they have not yet happened *to us*; perhaps it would be truer to say that we have not yet come to them. It will help us if we can grasp the idea that we are not in reality that point of consciousness—or rather, we are much more than that. We are *the whole line*, and the point of consciousness is passing from one part of ourselves to another part which is equally ourselves. It is within our possibilities to awaken the whole of ourselves, to be conscious of ourselves as a line and not merely as a point; and when we have succeeded in reaching that, we have transcended the delusion of *our* kind of time, for the past and the future lie simultaneously before us.

Take the analogy of a railway train, which we may suppose to be running from south to north. We move along that line and at any given moment we see what is visible from the particular point at which we happen to be. We remember as much as we have observed of the scenery through which we have passed; but we are ignorant of the scenery which lies before us, if it is our first journey along that line. We know, however, that the whole railway exists all the time, and that the objects which we see in succession are really simultaneously in existence; and it is not difficult for us to imagine a condition in which, by being simultaneously present at every point, we could have the whole panorama before us at the same time. By climbing a high mountain or ascending in a balloon we could to some extent realize this idea, except that in that case the point of view would be entirely changed and so the analogy would be imperfect.

But we have still to realize that there is quite another motion going on—one of which we are, normally, entirely unconscious. We may typify this by a lateral motion of the line—say from west to east. So that if we suppose all this motion to be taking place in a square, it would seem to us that our evolution consisted in a northward movement in a line parallel to the side of the square, and to attain the northern side would seem the end and object of that evolution. Yet the real goal is all the while not the northern side but the north-east corner, and there is another time moving at right angles to our time, which carries our past and our future with it just as surely as that fleeting illusion which we call our present. In the analogy of the railway, this time is typified by the rotation of the earth, which is all the while carrying the whole railway (with our train upon it) from west to east, though of this we know nothing by our physical sensations.

That other time is God's time; and in *that* time
what we call our past is not irrevocable, but is
constantly changing, though always in the direction
of improvement, or evolution. It may be said that
the events of the past cannot be changed; but
that statement is after all an assumption. The
important events of the past are our contacts with
other egos, our relation with them; and these
relations *are* being changed, whether we know it or
not; for they are in this direction at right angles to
what *we* call time, which at present we are unable
to appreciate.

But just as it is now possible for us to become
conscious all along our line instead of only at one
point of it, so will it in the far-away future be
possible for us to acquire a consciousness which
shall contain *the whole square*—a consciousness
equivalent to that which now seems to us the
Divine Consciousness. Probably then the whole
process will be repeated, and we shall find that the
whole square is moving at right angles to itself; but
it is better to try to grasp one facet of the idea at a
time. In the same way our railroad is not only being
carried round from west to east as the earth rotates
upon its axis, but it is also being carried through
space at a far swifter rate as the earth revolves
round the sun; and it has yet again an additional
and quite different motion as the whole solar system

revolves in its incalculable orbit round some far greater central sun.

This transcendental view of time has been very beautifully expressed by the late Mr. C. H. Hinton in his story *Stella*:

> If you felt eternity, you would know that you are never separated from anyone with whom you have ever been. You come to a different part of yourself every day, and you think the part that is separated in time is gone, but in eternity it is always there.
>
> If you felt eternity, you would know that what you did to a person and what he did to you is gradually changing. You think it is over and done with, but in eternity what you and he did to each other is always there and always changing and altering. As you grow better, he will act quite differently and you will act quite differently.
>
> If you felt eternity, you would know that you are always living in your *whole life*, that it is always changing, though with your eyes you can see only the part you are in now. The present is just a concentration like attending to one thing at a time.

> The Present is the child of the Past; the Future, the begotten of the Present. And yet, O present moment! knowest thou not that thou hast no parent, nor canst thou have a child; that thou art ever begetting but thyself? Before thou hast even begun to say: " I am the progeny of the departed moment, the child of the past," thou hast become that past itself. Before thou utterest the last syllable, behold! thou art no more the Present, but verily that Future. Thus are the Past, the Present, and the Future the Ever-living Trinity in one—the Mahamaya of the Absolute Is.—*The Secret Doctrine*, Vol. II, p. 466.

" Time " is only an illusion produced by the succession of our states of consciousness as we travel through Eternal Duration . . . The Present is only a mathematical line which divides that part of Eternal Duration which we call the Future, from that part which we call the Past. Nothing on earth has real duration . . . and the sensation we have of the actuality of the division of Time known as the Present, comes from the blurring of the momentary glimpse, or succession of glimpses, of things that our senses give us, as those things pass from the region of ideals, which we call the Future, to the region of memories that we name the Past . . . No one would say that a bar of metal dropped into the sea came into existence as it left the air, and ceased to exist as it entered the water, and that the bar itself consisted only of that cross-section thereof which at any given moment coincided with the mathematical plane that separates, and, at the same time, joins, the atmosphere and the ocean. Even so persons and things; which—dropping out of the " to be " into the " has been," out of the Future into the Past—present momentarily to our senses a cross-section, as it were, of their total selves, as they pass through Time and Space (as Matter) on their way from one eternity to another.—*The Secret Doctrine*, Vol. I, p. 69.

CHAPTER VI

INSPIRATION

As our consciousness begins to open to influences from higher worlds, we are likely to come more and more intimately into contact with the phenomenon called inspiration. In all great spiritual movements outpourings of force from higher planes have taken place, and there is no reason to suppose that the latest of such movements will vary in that respect from the older manifestations. Most of our members know that we had a remarkable example of such a downflow at one of the meetings of the Order of the Star, at Benares, on December 28th, 1911, and there must be many who have felt the same thing in a lesser degree at other meetings.

The whole subject of such inspiration, of such pouring out of influence, is one of great interest; one that it is profitable for us to try to comprehend. We talk habitually of inspiration, but it is not generally at all understood, and the word is used to cover phenomena of different types. The manifestation to which I have just referred, though entirely spontaneous and unexpected, partook to some extent of the nature of those periodical effluxes of power from above upon a number of people simultaneously, upon which religions largely rely for the helping and strengthening of their followers. These public and general inspirations, if we may call them so, are in themselves a subject of enthralling interest to which but little scientific attention has been devoted. I have recently made a careful study of it in connection with certain Christian services, and have published the results in a book called *The Science of the Sacraments*. I hope to see the same work undertaken by some qualified exponent for each of the great religions of the world; for it is a side of religious influence that has been much neglected, and it seems to me to be one of great importance.

It is not, however, of these endeavours to affect the collective consciousness of a congregation that I wish to write here, but rather of individual inspirations, and the possibility of our encountering them in the course of our progress. There is, however, another sense in which the word is used, to which it will be well first to make a passing reference.

The less intelligent among the Christians tell us that their scriptures are directly inspired by the Holy Ghost: many Christians hold to a general inspiration, which would prevent any serious error, but there are also many who carry it further and say that the actual words are so inspired. I am sorry to say that they sometimes make themselves ridiculous by carrying it further still, and saying that every word of the English translation must necessarily also be directly inspired by God. In fact, I fancy that many of the people who hold that view believe that the original messages were given in English! The nearest approach to rationality along this line is the theory that the same Holy Spirit who inspired the original writers also descended upon the translators and made them do their work with verbal accuracy.

I am afraid the verbal accuracy occasionally fails us, but there is this much to be said in favour of their idea, that the English translation of the Christian Scriptures is far finer in many respects than the original. If it ever comes in your way, as it did in mine as a student of divinity, to consult the original and compare it in considerable detail with the translation, I think you cannot but be struck, especially with regard to the Old Testament, with the fact that the original does not seem so poetical, so splendid in many respects, so beautiful and so musically expressed. There is some justification for the theory that King James' translators were the really inspired people, and those who know something of the influence which He whom we now call the Comte de St. Germain exercised over that translation, will be prepared to believe that there is a great deal of truth behind that theory of the rendering into such magnificent English of the scripture which was to have under that particular guise so world-wide an influence. If we compare the French translation of the Bible with the English, I think we shall agree that the former is a poor thing in comparison, and does not give at all the same effect—that our Christian brothers in France lose much by the fact that their scripture is by no means so poetically and so felicitously expressed as our own translation. Luther's translation into German is somewhat better, but even that, I think, falls much below the English version. I mean the old English authorized version; the revised version is more accurate in some respects, but in many cases it has lost the old poetry and the old inspiration.

But the reality of inspiration is not quite as orthodox people imagine it. Some Christians apparently believe that God the Holy Ghost dictated word by word those very scriptures, and are not at all disturbed by the fact that that is obviously untrue, as the books contain numerous mistakes. Yet, apart from such foolish belief, there is a vast amount of inspiration of different sorts going on, not perhaps from so high a source as the ill-instructed Christian supposes, but perfectly real inspiration nevertheless, even though it does not take just that form.

Any student of Theosophy must be aware that our Masters, the true Leaders of the Society, have frequently inspired its speakers and writers; but They have not done so, as a rule, by any sort of verbal dictation. Far more frequently They have done it by projecting into the mind of the speaker or writer certain ideas, leaving the man to clothe them in his own words. That is unquestionably an inspiration, because *spiro* means " I breathe "; so inspiration is something breathed into one from without, and those ideas in that sequence would not have occurred to the speaker or writer without that interference. Of that kind of inspiration I think we have had a great deal.

Those who have heard the lectures of our revered President can hardly fail to have been struck by the wonderful eloquence with which she speaks. That is of course native to her; it is a priceless talent which she holds in this life because she has won it by many lives of assiduous practice in public speaking. But one who hears her as often as I have done, many hundreds of times probably, will soon learn that besides her magnificent flights of elo-quence other and different forms of speech some-times fall from her lips, and that she is unquestion-ably sometimes guided from without as to what she shall say. I think she would herself say: "Sometimes I feel that my Master is putting ideas into my mind, and I simply express them"; she would even tell you that there have been occasions when He has actually used her organs and spoken through her Himself. I have myself heard that happen on several occasions, and the change is most marked. When left to herself our President speaks always in splendid flowing sentences. I have heard her say, when asked about her eloquence: "While I am speaking one sentence I see the next sentence in the air before me in two or three different forms, and I select from those that which I think will be most effective." I have no personal experience of that sort of thing; that talent has not been given to me; I have not this wonderful gift of eloquence. We use that expression, " a gift ", because as far as this life is concerned it is a gift; but remember that it is the result of work done in the past.

Those glowing periods, those balanced and modulated sentences—that is her style when left to herself; but her Master speaks usually in short, sharp sentences. In this incarnation, before He resigned His place in the world and became—not an ascetic exactly, but at least one who devotes the whole of His life entirely to spiritual work—He was a King in India, a commander of troops, accustomed to state exactly what He wanted in strong, brief, military sentences. He does so still, and it is striking indeed to watch the President's style suddenly change into the tone of command, to hear it alter from measured cadences to short, strong sentences—a most interesting study for a student of psychology. That is another form of inspiration.

Sometimes a spiritualist says to us: " In what way does such a condition as that which you thus describe differ from mediumship, to which, I am told, you have a decided objection? "

I answer that the difference is fundamental; the two conditions are wide as the poles asunder. In mediumship a person is passive, and lays himself open to the influence of any astral entity who happens to be in the neighbourhood. When under the influence he is usually unconscious, and knows neither what is being done through his organism nor who is doing it; he remembers nothing when he awakens from his trance. His state is really one of temporary obsession. There is generally supposed to be a dead man in charge of the proceedings, who is called a spirit-guide; but I have seen several cases in which such a guide proved utterly unable to afford efficient protection, for he encountered a force far stronger than his own, with results disastrous to his medium.

If one of our Masters chooses to speak through one of His pupils, the latter is fully conscious of

8

what is being done, and knows perfectly to whom he is for the moment lending his vocal organs. He stands aside from his vehicle, but he remains keenly alert and watchful; he hears every word that is uttered through him, follows with reverent interest all that occurs, and remembers everything clearly. There is nothing in common between the two cases, except that in both of them the body of one man is temporarily used by another.

Our Masters not infrequently make use of Their pupils, not always in speaking or writing only, but in quite other ways. In the great case at Benares on the 28th December nothing was spoken by Alcyone beyond a word or two of benediction at the end of the meeting—nothing more than that; but still the outpouring of the influence was clearly felt by many. It is the custom of the Master to pour influence through His pupil, and often that influence may be not such as we class under the term " inspiration "; that is to say, it will not prompt the pupil to do or to say anything whatever, but it will be simply a tremendous outpouring of spiritual force which may be employed for various purposes; sometimes for the healing of some disease, but more often for the comforting of some one who is in trouble, for the guidance of some one who is in great difficulty.

Perhaps that is one of the ways in which prayers are answered. Most students would say that prayer, in the ordinary sense of the word, is not a thing to which they attach great importance—not a thing which they would recommend. I myself feel, not only as a Theosophist but as a bishop of the Christian Church, that to pray to God for anything personal for oneself implies a lack of faith in Him; it distinctly implies that He needs to be told what is best for His people. I never felt myself so sure of what was best for me as to think that I was in a position to dictate to the Supreme Ruler of heaven and earth. It always seemed to me that He must know so far better than I, and that, being a loving Father (as I am absolutely certain that He is), He is already doing all for me that can be done, and needs no requests from me—more especially as my request might very likely be for something which I wish, though in reality it may not be at all the best thing for me. Therefore I have always felt that anything in the nature of personal prayer is to some extent an exhibition of distrust. I am so absolutely convinced that what is being done is beyond all question the best that can be done under all circumstances and taking everything into account, that it would never occur to me to ask the Great Architect of the Universe to alter His arrangements in order to suit me. I cannot think that such prayer is a commendable thing. I should consider meditation or aspiration a better form in which to express one's spiritual need.

But vast numbers of people do pray; and the Christians, the Hindus, the Muhammadans all agree in telling us that prayers are often answered. They *are*. It may be that theoretically they ought not to be, but they *are*, and it is useless for scientific investigators to blink facts. If prayers are sometimes answered, how does it happen? for of course we cannot suppose that the Supreme Ruler of the Universe turns aside in His scheme at the request of man. Who then hears these smaller prayers, and to some extent deals with them? Obviously lower entities of some sort. Our Roman Catholic friends tell us that each man has his guardian Angel, that there are great hierarchies of Angels always surrounding us, and that any one of these may be reached by a prayer, and may do in response to it whatever "in the providence of God," as they would say, he is permitted to do.

There is a great deal of truth in the idea. There are hosts of non-human beings peopling the space around us. As a general rule they have nothing to do with us nor we with them; but it is humanity that loses by that state of affairs, and it exists only because people know as a rule nothing about them. It would indeed be well for humanity that it should sometimes be helped by these greater people; and indeed even now it often is so helped without knowing it. I have given some instances of this in *Invisible Helpers*, and they are only examples; one could find hundreds more in which external assistance of one kind or another is given.

Some such cases of help are instances of the vigilance of those disciples of our Masters who are working constantly during sleep in the astral world; they see cases where they think some help can safely be given, and they step in and give it. Others show the interference of some non-physical being, but there is no evidence to show who the being was. It may have been what is commonly called a dead man, or it may have been one of those other non-human spirits; but the facts that such entities do surround us, and that now and then interference of some sort does take place—these are facts which we can verify for ourselves. We may read the published accounts of such interventions; we may look round and inquire whether any such instances can be found in the lives of those whom we know. Remember that we do not as a rule lay ourselves out at all for any such assistance, or for any suggestion from non-physical sources. Remember that the world around us is blankly unintelligent on such matters, and blatantly sceptical about them, and that those are clearly not

the conditions which would encourage such intervention.

But if we go to Catholic countries where people
do realize the possibility of such interventions, we
shall find that they much more often take place
there, simply because the people, believing in the
possibility, lay themselves open to it in various
ways. The ignorant sceptic always says: " These
things do not come to me, because of my superior
discrimination; I should at once see through the
fraud, whatever it may be." That is a foolish attitude
to take; and the reason which his vanity gives him
for his lack of experience is not the true one. The
sceptic erects a barrier round himself by his
aggressive unbelief—a barrier which it is not worth
the while of the non-physical entity to pierce; and
so he goes unhelped, and consequently does not
believe that anyone else can be helped. But such
help does undoubtedly come, and sometimes it takes
the form of inspiration.

It has often been my own experience, and I think
it will be that of many public lecturers and preach-
ers, that when speaking on any given subject new
ideas are suddenly put into one's mind. Sometimes
those come from one's ego, the higher self, who
takes an interest in the work which is being done
by the lower self, and contrives to flash down a
fragment of information; but also sometimes they

come quite distinctly from outside and from some-
body else. It does not at all follow that the suggestions are necessarily in every respect accurate.
They represent the opinion of the person who gives
the suggestion, and a person in the astral world is no
more infallible than one in the physical world. Here
on this plane, if we heard a person talking about
some subject, and had the opportunity without seem-
ing intrusive, we should probably suggest to him
anything that we knew on the matter. We hear a
person explaining something to others, perhaps,
and we observe some gaps in his explanation which
we happen to be able to fill. If we are on friendly terms with that person, so that we can do it
without hurting his feelings, we shall make our
contribution in order that the instruction given may
be fuller and better. Just as we should do that in a
friendly way on the physical plane, so does the dead
man, so does the Angel, from the astral plane.

Many students of the occult have passed over
into the other world, but naturally they still retain
their interest not only in the subjects which they
studied, but in their own friends who are studying
them. They still come back and attend meetings
and lectures, and if an idea occurs to them on the
subject under consideration which is not in the
mind of the speaker or the lecturer, they will
endeavour to insert such an idea. They do not

materialize (which would be a great waste of force)
in order to get up and speak themselves, but they
can without much difficulty put the idea into a mind
which is already in sympathy with them, and that
is often done. Some entirely new idea, some fresh
illustration, is as it were thrust before the mind of
the speaker. He may think, especially if he does
not know much about the matter, that this is his
own cleverness, that he himself has invented this
new illustration. It does not matter. The point is
to get the idea put before the people; the entity
does not care who gets the credit of it, naturally
enough. So there is a great deal of inspiration
about, even now, and there might be much more if
people had an intelligent grasp of the subject, and
if they laid themselves out for such inspiration.

It will frequently happen to a man who is writing
an article, that these new ideas will come into his
mind. He has no means of knowing whether they
are his own ideas sent down by the ego, or thoughts
sent down by some other agency; but after all it
does not matter; there is no question of plagiarism
here. Whoever gives them, gives them voluntarily.
Any man preparing a subject should prepare it
meditatively, with his mind open to new impressions; and he will often get those impressions. What
of our poets? A poet is generally a man who is open
to impressions. Whence those impressions come

matters but little, so long as the ideas themselves are good. They may come from other poets who have passed over; they may come from Angels: they may come from his own higher self. What does it signify, so long as the thoughts are good and beautiful? They are sent down for him to utilize but it must not be forgotten that it is his responsibility to see that the ideas *are* good and true.

If a man accepts every idea which comes to him, he may truly claim that he is acting under inspiration, but he will often find that the inspiration is not a reliable one, because he cannot as a rule know the source from which it comes. There are cases in, which a man does know perfectly well. Those of us who have the privilege—the stupendous privilege—of communication with some of our Masters, soon come to know at once Their touch, Their magnetic influence, and so to recognize immediately when an idea comes to us from Them. Such ideas we should of course accept with the deepest reverence; but be very sure of their source, for there are those who are eager to deceive, and diabolically clever at the work of misrepresentation.

Remember, too, that anybody, with the best possible intentions, may put before us ideas which are not correct. A man is no more infallible because he happens to be dead, than he was when he happened to be alive. He is the same man. He certainly has now the *opportunity* of learning more than he knew before, but not every man takes his opportunities in that world any more than in this. One meets numbers of people who have been for twenty years in the astral world, and yet know no more than when they left this physical life, just as there are many people who have lived through fifty, sixty or seventy years of human life, and have contrived to imbibe remarkably little wisdom in the process. The advice or suggestion of those who have taken advantage of their opportunities is worth a great deal, whether it is given from the astral world or the physical world; but the two admonitions stand absolutely parallel, and we must attach no more importance to communications from the astral world, or from any higher plane, than we should to a suggestion made on the physical plane. We ought to be equally willing to receive them both, and we should attach to them just such importance as we feel they intrinsically deserve—that and no more, whencesoever they may come.

Inspiration is not infrequent: neither is that other form of influence of which I spoke—the spiritual force which is poured through a man who is in connection with a Great One. That also takes place quite often: and it is not only our own Masters who make use of physical people in that way. Other entities of all sorts may have their channels, through whom their force is poured out, and a great deal may be done in the world either by those who are dead or by those who belong to other systems of evolution than our own—those whom the Indians call Devas, whom in the West we know as Angels.

To take the ordinary sceptical or indifferent attitude would in many cases shut one off from the possibility of learning a great deal about these higher matters. When we come back to the more childlike attitude, which is at least receptive, though it may not be critical, we shall certainly find that there are possibilities of which now in our self-sufficiency we hardly dream.

Inspiration is a mighty reality, and so is the possibility of the outpouring of helpful force. Those who come into daily contact with it know well how constantly these things take place; and the blank prejudice against them, the sceptical attitude taken by so many people, is a source of wonder and pain to those who know, because it would seem as though men were intentionally, of malice prepense, shutting themselves away from one of the most interesting aspects of life—from one that may often be useful and helpful beyond all expectation.

Let us keep, then, an open mind with regard to such things. Inspiration may come to *us*; helpful force in some measure may flow through *us*. Let us be ready to be utilized in that way if our

karma is so good that we can be so utilized; and
when we see evidence that the same thing is
happening through others, again let us keep an open
mind, and not shut ourselves up in our own prejudice agaist the possibility of being helped and
guided. That, I think, is the best line that we can
take with regard to it.

Of course the other side needs emphasis too.
We should not too readily believe that which comes.
We must take everything on its own merits, no
matter though it appears to us to come from a great
Master—from a source to which we look for inspiration and for help. Even then, we must weigh it
always on its own merits, because these higher planes
are full of pitfalls to those who are unaccustomed to
them. It is always possible that a higher power
may be imitated by a lower one; it is possible that
there may be some one who is jealous of the influence
over us of a greater soul, some one who may take
the shape for the moment of that greater soul, and
endeavour to mislead us. It has happened often—
terribly often; and we have seen the saddest results
from it. Therefore the one and only safe ground is
to keep our minds open. It is foolish rashly to reject,
but equally foolish blindly to accept, merely because
the message comes to us with a high name attached,
or with an influence which seems to us to be beautiful.
Most things from other planes seem beautiful to us

down here, just because they come from a higher level, and bring with them something of its greater luminosity, of its more delicate vibrations, and of all the glamour of the inner world.   As St. Paul said long ago, every man should be fully persuaded in his own mind; he should try the spirits and what comes from them, whether they be of God.   Let us see for ourselves by all means, but do not let us shut out the possibility of influence by prejudging the whole question, and saying that inspiration is an affair of thousands of years ago, and can never take place now and here in the present day.

CHAPTER VII

PLAGIARISM

WHEN our consciousness develops sufficiently to enable us to understand a little of the working of Nature on the higher planes, we soon find it necessary to revise our judgment in various directions. As we comprehend conditions better, we see the reason for many things which previously seemed unaccountable, and we learn to make allowances for actions which we had before considered inexcusable. In this and the following chapter I am endeavouring to present some thoughts which have occurred to me along these lines.

In the newspapers lately have appeared reports of two legal actions for plagiarism in connection with stories or plays, and in each case the defendant declared that he had not read the work which he was accused of imitating. A man of the world would probably find it difficult to credit such a disclaimer, especially if the points of resemblance between the two stories or plays were many; yet the student of Occultism knows that such a plea may be perfectly true, and that there are more

ways than one in which such a coincidence may
happen without the slightest intention or consciousness of plagiarism on the part of anybody concerned.

In the second volume of *The Inner Life* I have
already explained that in the mental world there
are certain definitely localized thought-centres—that
thoughts of the same type are drawn together by
the similitude of their vibrations, just as men who
speak the same language are drawn together.
Philosophical thought, for example, has a distinct
realm of its own, with subdivisions corresponding
to the chief philosophical ideas, and all sorts of
curious inter-relations subsisting between these
various centres, exhibiting the way in which different systems of philosophy have linked themselves
together. Anyone who thinks deeply on philosophical subjects thereby brings himself into touch with
this group of vortices; if he is asleep or dead—that
is, if he is away from the limitations of his physical
body—he is drawn spatially to that part of the
mental plane; if the lump of earth to which he is
attached for the moment prevents that, he rises
into a condition of sympathetic vibration with one
or other of those vortices, and receives from them
whatever he is capable of assimilating, though
somewhat less freely than if he actually drifted to it.

This collection of ideas represents all that has
been thought upon that subject, and is therefore in

itself far more than enough for any ordinary thinker, yet there are further possibilities behind it and in connection with it which are within the reach of the few who are strong enough and persevering enough to penetrate to them.

First, through those centres of thought the living minds of those who generated their force may be reached, and so the modern thinker who is at once strong and eager, yet reverent and teachable, may actually sit at the feet of the great thinkers of the past, and learn how the problems of life envisaged themselves to the mightiest intellects which our world has produced.

Secondly, there is such a thing as the Truth in itself—or we may perhaps put, as the representative to us of such an utterly abstract idea, the conception of that Truth in the mind of our Solar Deity— surely a notion sufficiently lofty for the boldest. The man who has attained conscious union with the Deity is able to contact this thought, but no one below that level can reach it. Reflections of it are to be seen, cast from plane to plane, and growing ever dimmer as they descend; and some at least of these reflections are within the reach of the man whose thought can soar up like a strong eagle to meet them.

It is obvious that many earnest thinkers may simultaneously be drawn to the same mental region, and may there gather exactly the same ideas; and when that happens it is at least possible that their expression of those ideas in the physical world may also coincide; and then there is always the danger that the ignorant multitude may accuse one or the other of them of plagiarism. That this synchronous expression does not happen more frequently is due to the density of men's brains, which rarely allow their owners to bring through clearly anything which has been learned upon higher levels. Not only in the field of literature does synchronal manifestation occur; officials connected with the Patent Office of any country will tell us that applications with regard to practically identical inventions often arrive simultaneously; and when this fact is disclosed each of the applicants is very ready to accuse the other of stealing his ideas, even where physical theft is obviously impossible.

It is not, however, among the promulgators of philosophical ideas that we most frequently hear complaints of plagiarism, but rather among dramatists and writers of fiction. Is there, then, in connection with this form of literature any such thought-centre as we have just described in relation to philosophy? Not precisely—at any rate not for fiction as a whole. But there is a region for what may be called romantic thought—a vast but rather ill-defined group of forms, including on one side a

9

host of vague but brilliant combinations connected with the relation of the sexes, on another the emotions characteristic of mediæval chivalry and the legends illustrating them, and on yet another masses of fairy stories.

Many writers of certain kinds of fiction and poetry derive much inspiration from excursions into these regions; others come into contact with the shoreless ocean of past history. No untrained person can actually read the records of that history, for that needs the full awakening of the ego, so that he can function in the atomic matter of his causal body. But confused reflections of the more brilliant episodes from those records are thrown down to lower mental levels, and even into the astral world, and those may readily be contacted by wandering voyagers in there realms. So it happens that many a writer finds himself in possession of a splendid idea, a dramatic climax perhaps, and he builds a story to lead up to it, and gains much fame thereby, never knowing all the while that he is but relating a tiny fragment of the world's true history.

Years ago, on board a steamer, I myself read a remarkable novel—one with a plot absolutely out of the ordinary run—and I mentally applauded the ingenuity of the author, though even then it stirred within me a vague remembrance which told me that some reality lay behind it. I did not pursue the subject, and it was only comparatively recently, in following out the history of a series of past incarnations, that I came across the fact of which this story was the expression . Yet neither I, who recorded in those lives the incident as it occurred, nor the novelist who had expanded it into a charming story, was in the least guilty of plagiarism, any more than a traveller who visits and describes the beauties of the River Rhine is guilty of a plagiarism from Baedeker.

In some cases the writer of fiction does not need to search the higher worlds for plots and ideas, for these are provided for him ready-made. One leading novelist of the day has himself told me that his stories come to him he knows not whence—that they are in reality written not by him but through him. In this case the writer understands and recognizes the state of affairs; but I believe that there are many other writers in the same case who are blankly unconscious of it. We know so little what is our own (if indeed anything ever is); for not only may we roam the realms of thought and pick up unconsidered trifles on our journey, but others may do for us the roaming and the collection, and we may be nothing but their mouthpiece, even while we marvel at the rapidity and lucidity with which new ideas (new to us, at least) are pouring forth from our brains.   Those who during earth-life have written on any subject retain their interest in it after the casting-off of the physical body. In their new and less trammelled life they see sides of it which before were imperceptible to them, they obtain broader views of it, because their whole horizon is widened. As they continue their study under these far better conditions, new light dawns upon it as upon all else, because of their greatly enhanced power of vision; and often they yearn to put their newer and greater conceptions before their fellow men.

But in that new life there are restrictions as well as opportunities; they can learn far more if they will, but they can no longer obtain a physical publisher for their lucubrations. If they wish to reach this lower world they must do so through some one living in it. Here arise difficulties in their way—difficulties which most of them never learn how to overcome. Some few do, and succeed in getting their ideas before the world which they have left, but only under the name of some other man, and often very imperfectly. Naturally enough, the unconscious medium through whom they work mingles their ideas with his own, and colours them with his idiosyncrasies. In some cases the brain upon which alone they find themselves able to work is incapable of transmitting the full value of the thought which they try to pour into it; and in some

cases defective education or lack of special knowledge stands in the way of perfect transmission. I
very clearly remember, for example, the annoyance
and the impatience of old Mr. Cayley when he
endeavoured to give to the world through me some
new discovery which he declared would revolutionize
the whole science of mathematics. As I unfortunately know very little of that science, I was quite
unable to understand what he was talking about,
and so I was compelled to forego the honour which
he destined for me; but I must admit that his
language was distinctly uncomplimentary, and I
can quite understand that his disappointment may
have been keen, as he told me that he had already
tried many of his colleagues in vain.

Yet the fact remains that we have but little title
to much which we think to be our own. Goethe
wrote:

What would remain to me if the art of appropriation
were derogatory to genius? Every one of my writings
has been furnished to me by a thousand different persons,
a thousand things, wise and foolish have brought me,
without suspecting it, the offering of their thoughts,
faculties and experience. My work is an aggregation of
beings taken from the whole of nature; it bears the
name of Goethe.

If the great German admits this to be so with
regard to the splendid sunlight of his genius, how
much more must it be true of the farthing rushlights

of minor writers! It is sometimes not only the ideas that are borrowed, but even the forms of expression; I have seen instances in which two people entirely unconnected put down the same thought in the very same words. This may be due to the zeal and enthusiasm of some dead man; he dictates the same sentence to two or more people, because he is not certain which of them will be able to carry it through successfully to the physical plane. It may, however, also happen without the intervention of a dead man, for an author himself, when assimilating some thought, often finds it less troublesome to take it exactly as it stands than to find for it a new expression in words of his own. In all these matters the natural tendency is to flow along the line of least resistance, and the line of least resistance is that which is already established.

It is very difficult to give, to one who has not seen them, any idea of the appearance of such reservoirs of thought as I have been attempting to describe. One might partially image it by saying that each thought makes for itself a track—burrows out a way for itself through the matter of the plane; and that way, when once established, remains open for the treading—or rather, it may readily be re-opened and its particles re-vivified by any fresh effort. If this effort be at all in the general direction of that old line of thought, it is far easier for it to adapt itself sufficiently to pass along that line than it is for it to hew out for itself a slightly different line, however closely parallel that may be to what already exists.

All these considerations show us that it is not wise to hurl reckless accusations of plagiarism at the heads of those who happen to express themselves much as we have done—or even exactly as we have done. I have sometimes seen a certain impatience manifested among Theosophists because writers or speakers who are not members of our Society frequently use what we call Theosophical ideas without any acknowledgement of their source. As there are quarters in which the name of Theosophy is unpopular, I have little doubt that this is sometimes intentionally done, and credit withheld from the Society in order to avoid the mention of the hated name. Even in that case, however, I cannot see that we as Theosophists need complain, for our one wish is to circulate the teaching of the truth, not to obtain credit for the knowledge of it.

There are, however, a number of other cases in which information about truths well known to us is acquired quite outside our organization. For example, we have been at some pains to map out the subdivisions of the astral and mental planes, and to describe their inhabitants and the conditions which prevail there; but we must remember that all living people pass on to the astral plane during sleep, and that dead people permanently reside there during the earlier stage of the *post-mortem* life; so it must inevitably happen that among these many millions of people some will be sufficiently sensitive either when alive to bring back into physical existence some clear recollections, or when dead to discover some method of communicating reasonably accurate information to those whom they have left behind. Whenever one of these things happens, we immediately have what we are in the habit of calling a confirmation of Theosophical teaching. But this is in no sense of the word a plagiarism; it is an independent observation of the same phenomenon, and the observer has just as much right to describe his impressions as I should have to give mine of a visit to Italy, even though there are already many hundreds of books upon that country far better than anything that I could write. I have no wish to defend plagiarism, which is indeed nothing but a form of robbery. I wish merely to point out that it is not well to make reckless accusations along that line, since the conditions of the holding of property upon higher planes are very different from those which obtain in the physical world, and in this case, as in so many others, the man who most fully understands is also the man who will take the most charitable view.

CHAPTER VIII

EXAGGERATION

WE all know people who have a tendency to exaggerate—who never can relate an incident exactly as it happened or pass on a story without improving upon it. After a time we get used to them, and learn to allow a certain discount off everything which they say. Usually we regard them as untruthful, and often also as conceited, especially if their magnifications refer (as they generally do) chiefly to their own part in the stories which they tell.

A considerable amount of experience, however, with those who have this peculiarity has convinced me that in most cases the exaggeration is unconscious. A person finds himself in a certain position, and in that position he (being in all probability quite an ordinary man) acts or speaks much as any average human being would do. In thinking over the situation afterwards, he often realizes that he might have met that little emergency much more effectively and dramatically—that he might have covered himself with glory by making some particularly apposite remark, if only it had occurred to him at the time. If he happens to be the type of man who cannot put aside an event when it is past, and forget it in a sane and healthy manner, he continues to brood over the trifling incident and reconstruct it, imagining how the conversation would have proceeded if he had made what he now sees to be the most effective retort, or how the drama would have worked itself out if he had not lost his head (as so many of us do) just at the critical moment. And after he has rehearsed the occurrence a few times along these lines, he begins actually to believe that he really did make that splendidly witty remark, or that he was in fact that hero of romance which he feels that he ought to have been, and indeed would have been if only he had thought of it.

Such a man is no doubt acutely self-conscious, otherwise he would not continue to worry himself about an event which is past and cannot be recalled; and he has also a certain amount of imagination and sensitiveness. The former quality enables him to make strong thought-forms of himself as doing or saying what he feels ought to have been done or said, while the latter quality enables him to sense these thought-forms and to feel their reaction upon him until he fails to distinguish them from the actual memory of the event; and so after a time he relates in all good faith a story which departs widely from the facts as recollected by a more prosaic spectator. Indeed, I have myself on more than one occasion been put in a most awkward position by being appealed to in public to confirm a highly-coloured account of some experience which the narrator and I had shared in the past, but in regard to which my recollection was distinctly less dramatic than that of my poetically inclined partner. I have even in some cases had the interesting experience of watching a story grow—having in the first place myself witnessed what really happened, and heard the principal actor give at the time a reasonably exact account of it. Coming back a week later, I have found that the tale had considerably expanded; and after a few months it had even become wholly unrecognizable, the embroidery of self-glorification having completely disguised its substratum of fact. Yet I am sure that this inaccuracy is wholly unintentional, and that the narrator who is so entirely misrepresenting the story has no thought of deceiving us, and indeed would shrink with horror from any deliberate falsification.

This is a curious phenomenon; and although, in the extreme form which I have described, it is fortunately confined to comparatively few, we may all of us detect what may be regarded as a sort of germ of it in ourselves. Many of us find it difficult to be absolutely accurate; we are conscious of a certain desire to make a story more dramatically complete than it is in reality—to round it off, or to introduce into it the element of poetic justice which is so often sadly lacking in the very limited views which alone we are able to take of mundane affairs. Quite a number of people who have every intention of being perfectly truthful will yet, if they watch themselves carefully, find that they are not entirely free from this curious instinct of magnification— that in repeating a story they instinctively increase the size or the distance or the value of that of which they speak.

Why does this tendency exist? It is no doubt true that in many cases there is something of conceit, of desire for approbation, of the wish to shine or to appear clever; and even where these terms would be too strong, there is an instinctive self-consciousness which causes the person concerned to look back to past events in which he took part, with the desire that that part had been more distinguished. Yet quite apart from that, and where the story has no connection with ourselves, we still perceive the same curious tendency.

The reason lies deeper than that; and in order to understand it we must think of the nature of the ego, and of the stage which he has reached in his evolution. It has often been mentioned in our literature that one of the characteristics of the ego is his remarkable power of dramatization. In another chapter I endeavoured to explain that he deals with abstractions as we on the physical plane deal with concrete acts—that to him a whole system of philosophy (with all that it involves) is a single idea which he uses as a counter in his game, which he throws down in the course of a conversation, just as we down here might quote a fact in support of some contention which we were urging. Thus we see that, when dealing with matters on his own plane and those below him, all his ideas are complete ideas, properly rounded off and perfect. Anything incomplete would be unsatisfactory to him—would in fact hardly be counted as an idea at all. For him a cause includes its effect, and therefore, in the longer view which he is able to take, poetic justice is always done, and no story can ever end badly. These characteristics of his reflect themselves to a certain extent in his lower vehicles, and we find them appearing in ourselves in various ways. Children always demand that their fairy-tales shall end well, that virtue shall be rewarded and that vice shall be vanquished; and all unsophisticated and healthy-minded people feel a similar desire. Those who (on the pretext that things do not happen this way in real life) clamour for an evil realism are precisely those whose views of life have become unhealthy and unnatural, because in their short-sighted philosophy they can never see the whole of any incident, but only the fragment of it which shows in one incarnation—and usually only the merest outside husk even of that.

Let us notice the influence exercised upon the manifestation of this characteristic by the stage of evolution at which we now are. It has often been explained that each root-race has its special quality to develop, and that in that respect each of the sub-races also manifests the influence of its own special peculiarity upon the root-race quality. The Fourth Root-Race, we are told, was chiefly concerned with the development of the astral body and of its emotions, while our Fifth Root-Race is supposed to be evolving the mental body and the intellect which is intended to work through it. Thus in the fifth or Teutonic sub-race we should be intensifying the development of intellect and discrimination, whereas in the fourth or Keltic sub-race we may see how its combination makes easier both artistic and psychic development, though probably at the cost of scientific accuracy in detail. In fact, this passion for scientific accuracy, for perfect truth in minutest detail, is comparatively a recent development; indeed, it is that characteristic which has made possible the achievements of modern science. We now demand first of all that a thing shall be true, and if it is not, it is of no interest to us; whereas the older sub-races demanded first of all that it should be pleasing, and declined to be limited in their appreciation by any such consideration as whether the thing had ever materialized or could ever materialize on the physical plane.

You may see this clearly in the old Keltic stories. Notice how in the legends which cluster round King Arthur, a knight tilts with some casual stranger, overthrows him and brings him as a prisoner, and how, in narrating his exploit, he describes his unlucky victim as a gigantic ogre, a monster towering to the skies, and so on; and yet nobody present appears to notice any discrepancy between his account and the actual appearance of the unfortunate person then and there before them. We see at once, as we read those stories, that for their reciters and their hearers the limitations of what we call facts simply did not exist. Their one desire was to make up a good and soul-satisfying romance, and in this they succeeded. That the alleged occurrence was manifestly impossible did not trouble them in the slightest degree. It troubles us who read these fables now, because we are developing the discriminative faculty, and therefore, though we like a rousing tale of adventure just as well as our forefathers did, we cannot feel satisfied with it unless an air of probability is cleverly thrown around each

incident to satisfy this new yearning for verisimili-
tude and accuracy of statement.

This desire for accuracy is only the coming
through of another of the qualities of the ego—his
power to see truly, to see a thing as it is—as a whole
and not only in part. But because down here we
are so often unable to see the whole as he sees it,
we are beginning to demand that the part which we
do see shall be to a certain extent complete in itself,
and shall harmonize with such other parts as we can
dimly glimpse. Our little fragments are usually very
far from complete. They do not end properly,
they do not show off the characters to the best
advantage; and because down here we cannot yet
see the real ending which would explain everything,
our instinct is to inset an imaginary ending which at
least to some extent meets our requirements.

That is the real reason for our desire to
improve upon a story. In some of us the newly
developed desire for truth and accuracy overpowers
the older craving to please and be pleased; but
sometimes the other element is victorious. Then
comes in, as we have already said, the influence of
vanity and the desire to make a good appearance,
and our newly developed quality of truthfulness
falls ignominiously into the background. In most
cases all this takes place entirely in the subconscious
mind, and so our ordinary waking consciousness is

unaware of it. Thus it comes about that some
people are still quite mediaeval in their accounts of
their personal adventures.

When we understand this, it is clearly our
business to assist the ego in his present efforts at
development. We must encourage and insist on the
quality of accuracy, and we must keep our record of
facts apart from our thoughts and wishes with
regard to those facts. Yet in thus cultivating truthfulness we need by no means extinguish romance.
It is necessary to be accurate; it is not necessary to
become a Gradgrind. If we wish to pass an examination in botany we must load our memories with
uncouth, pseudo-Latinized terms, and we must
learn to distinguish the dicotyledonous from the
monocotyledonous; but that need not prevent us
from recognizing that there is a higher side to
botany in which we study the existence of the life
of the tree and its power occasionally to manifest in
quasi-human form, nor need we ignore the folk-lore
of the trees and plants and the action of the nature-
spirits who help in the moulding and the colouring
of the blossoms—though we shall do well to keep all
these rigidly out of our examination papers. The
knowledge of the beauty and romance which lies
behind need not be lost because we have to acquire
arid, superficial details, any more than we need lose
sight of the fact that sugar is sweet and pleasant to

10

the taste because we have to learn that its chemical formula is $C_{12}H_{22}O_{11}$.

To mingle our imagination with our facts is a wrong use of a very mighty power; but there is a right use of it which may be of great help to us in our progress.   One who desires to meditate is often told to make an image of the Master and fix his attention upon it; and when he does this, the love and devotion which he feels attract the attention of the Master, and He immediately fills that image with His thought, and pours through it His strength and His blessing upon its creator.   If the student has been fortunate enough to see the Master, his thought-image is naturally far clearer and better than in cases where it is a mere effort of the imagination. The clearer the image, the more fully can power be sent through it; but in any and every case something at least is gained, and some considerable return is received. This then is a case of the legitimate use of the imagination—a case in which its results are most valuable.

It comes into play also in one of the many lines of psychic development. A pupil who desires to open the etheric sight is sometimes told to take some solid object and endeavour to imagine what the inside of it would be like if he could see it. For example, a closed box might be set before such a pupil, and he might be asked to

describe the objects inside it. He would probably
be directed to try to imagine what was inside, to
" guess," as the children would say, but always with
an effort of strained attention, with an endeavour to
see that which by ordinary sight he could not see.
It is said that after many such attempts the pupil
finds himself " guessing " correctly much more
frequently than is explicable on any theory of
coincidence, and that presently he begins really to
see before him the objects which at first he only
imagined.

A variant of this practice is that the student
calls up before his mind's eye the room of a friend
and endeavours to make a perfect image of it. After
a certain number of attempts he will probably be
able to do this readily, and with considerable wealth
of detail. Then he should watch closely for anything new or unusual in his mind-picture of that
room; or perhaps he may be conscious of the
presence of certain people in it. If that happens
to him it may be worth his while to write and ask
whether such people have been there, or whether
there is any foundation for his idea that certain
changes have been made; for if he proves to be
right on a number of occasions he will realize that
he is beginning to develop a certain impressibility
which may in process of time evolve into true
clairvoyance.

To sum up: Like other powers, imagination may be used rightly or wrongly. Exaggeration is clearly wrong, and is always a bar to progress, even when it is unintentional. Accuracy is essential; but its achievement does not preclude the study of the higher and more romantic side of nature.

CHAPTER IX

MEDITATION

THE readiest and safest method of developing the higher consciousness is by means of meditation, and it is already the habit of many of our members to begin each morning by spending a few minutes in a meditation which is intended to be devoted to aspiration towards the Masters. I should like to say a few words about this, because it seems to me that some of us are not getting quite as much out of it as we might do.

There are so many various types among us that it is not possible that one method of meditation can produce equally good results with all. Broadly speaking, we may divide into two classes the ways in which such a time as that may be most profitably occupied, and each person must decide for himself or herself to which class he or she belongs, which method will come most naturally and be most profitable.

We have the habit of calling all our exercises of that sort by the general name of meditation, though it is appropriate only to some of them. I have often spoken of three stages through which people have to pass: Concentration, Meditation, and Contemplation; it is this last at which on the whole we ought to be aiming, when that is possible and comparatively easy for us. There may be, however, some of us whose minds are not constructed along that particular line, and they may find meditation more useful and more profitable for them.

The art of acquiring perfect concentration is a slow process, and most of us are only in process of acquiring it. We have not fully succeeded in it yet, because wandering thoughts still come in to trouble us. But supposing we have sufficient concentration to keep out those thoughts which we do not want, it yet remains to be considered how we shall think during these few minutes. We speak of the time as devoted to aspiration towards the Master; but there are different lines of aspiration. The nearest to what is really meant by meditation would be to hold the mind firmly upon our own image of Him, if we are able to construct a good strong thought-image. Some cannot visualize as easily as others. If we can visualize strongly for ourselves, it is well to make our own thought-image and close our eyes. Having made such an image, our thought would then run along some such line as this:

"This," we should say, "is the Master whom I have chosen, to whom I am devoting myself. He is the incarnation of love, of power, of wisdom. I must try to make myself like Him in all these respects. Have I succeeded so far in doing this? Not as fully as I should wish in such-and-such ways; I can think, in looking back, that I have not shown these qualities as I should. I shall endeavour in the future to remember Him always, and to be, and to act, and to think as I believe He would be and act and think." And so on with a strong effort to realize those qualities in Him. I take it that that is really what is meant by the word meditation.

If a man finds after some effort that it is impossible for him to make a clear thought-image, it will be well for him to seat himself before a portrait of the Master, and fix his gaze earnestly upon it while thinking as above suggested.

There is something still better, perhaps, for those who find that they can do it readily and easily; and that is contemplation. In that case one forms the image of the Master and, having formed it, throws one's whole strength into an effort to reach Him, an effort which I can best describe by saying that we are straining upwards towards Him, trying to unify our consciousness with His. That effort will not immediately bring a result, in all probability; but if we make it every day in our regular meditation, the time will certainly come when it will meet with full success.

That is the best thing to do for those who can do it. But there are types of mind to which such an effort would be barren; and it is not well for them to waste their time over it if it is a thing which they cannot at all do, while the other form of meditation might be much more fruitful for them.

But for those who can reach upward in that particular way with any sort of success, with any kind of feeling that it is for them a path which will be likely (even though it should take a long time) to lead to a direct union with Him, contemplation is clearly best, for such union when attained is most fruitful, most helpful. With deepest reverence we say to the Master:

"Holy Master, Father, Friend, I lay myself open to Your influence. It shall flow into me to the uttermost degree in which I am capable of receiving it."

We need not *ask* Him to pour it out on us, because He is doing that all the time. We do not *pray* to the Masters to do this or that. They know very much more about it than we do, and are already doing all that can be done; but it is on our side necessary that we should make ourselves open to it, that we should remove the barriers of self that stand in the way. That is the old story. It must be told over and over again, because the separated self is the one great difficulty in our path—

the personality first and then the individuality. That is insisted upon in *At the Feet of the Master*, and in every book that has been written on occult progress. When there is anything hindering our progress it is always the lower self which stands in the way of the Great Self.

Having visualized and realized the Master as intensely as possible, the effort must be to clear away our own barriers, to break through them and reach up to Him, because He is ever ready to be gracious to us, always pouring out His influence just in such measure as we are capable of receiving. We have nothing to ask Him. We have only so to deal with ourselves that His light shall shine through.

That effort will eventually lead us towards an extension of consciousness. When we succeed we shall break through into a different world, a different way of looking at everything. Along that line is the most rapid and the most satisfactory progress, but as I have said, it is strictly for those who can take it, and for whom that happens to be the way. The man whose nature instinctively runs the other way would probably waste his time by making this effort, whereas he might make distinct progress following that other line.

One or other of those things we ought to be trying to do, and we must not let it become vague. It has a great tendency to become vague; and it is

odd that although we believe that all these advance-
ments are within reach, we are never so much
astonished as when anything happens, and we do
really get any result. That ought not to be so. It
is no doubt a touching example of our humility, but
there is a humility that sometimes actually hinders
progress. We may feel sure that we are far away
from the possibility of doing anything, that we stand
in our own light. It is better, so far as may be,
with humble confidence (humble unquestionably,
but still confidence) to take the line: " Others have
succeeded in this. I intend to succeed, ar   am
going to persevere until I do."

Then we certainly shall succeed. It may not be
immediately, but " immediately " from our point of
view matters very little really, so long as we do the
thing; and every human being *can* do it; it is only
a question of the time it may happen to take, and
the time is well spent anyhow.

I think if we remember these ideas it may help
us to make more use of the time set apart for meditation. The natural tendency of the age generally
is towards vagueness and looseness of thought. Some
people just relapse into what is called" feeling good "
for a few minutes. Better to feel good than to feel
bad, of course; but still it is not quite all that is meant.

Many people meditate daily alone, and obtain
great help by so doing; but nevertheless there are

even greater possibilities of result when a group of people concentrate their minds on the one thing. That sets up a strain in the physical ether as well as in the astral and mental worlds, and it is a twist in the direction which we desire. For once, just for the time of that group meditation, instead of having to fight against our surroundings (which we always have to do practically, everywhere else) we find them actually helpful. That is to say, they ought to be so, if all present succeed in holding their minds from wandering, and that of course they must try to do, not only for their own sakes but for the sake of their comrades in the effort. A wandering mind in such a group constitutes a break in the current. Instead of having a huge mass of thought moving in one mighty flood, we should in that case have little eddies in it, such as are made by rocks or snags in a river which deflect the water. Anyone who allows his mind to wander is thereby making things not quite so easy for those around him.

A number of people all sending their thoughts in the same direction offer a fine opportunity for progress if the direction is a good one; but it rarely happens in ordinary life. When it does occur, it means great possibilities.

A striking instance, which I have described before, arises in my mind as apposite. I had the privilege of being present at the Diamond Jubilee of Her

Majesty Queen Victoria. It was one of the most
wonderful manifestations in the way of occult force
that I ever saw. Just for a few moments, as the
Queen's carriage passed, thousands of people were
swept into one line of thought, and it was a very
good line, of intense love and loyalty. It was a
sight from the inner side which is rarely equalled.
Before that came, we had to wait a long time for the
procession. Thousands and thousands of people
who were within sight had each his own set of
thoughts. I happened to be in the heart of the city
of London, where those present were mostly com-
mercial or professional men with their wives. The
men were chiefly occupied in calculations, and
their heads were surrounded by figures, just like
a swarm of bees flying round them all the time.
The various ladies were thinking about one another's
dresses and about domestic affairs of all sorts.
There was no unity, as is always the case with any
crowd anywhere.

When the procession came along, the people were
awakened, and by degrees began to take a stronger
and stronger interest in it, and the culmination
arrived when the Queen herself passed. For a few
minutes all those thousands were thinking and
feeling alike. The effect was quite prodigious even
on the physical plane, though they did not know
why. Here were hard city men, absolutely with

tears in their eyes, shaking each other by the hand; while practically all the ladies were weeping unrestrainedly.

The effect was amazing in those few minutes of utter exaltation. Perhaps for the first time in their lives they all of them simultaneously forgot themselves altogether, and were lifted right out of themselves by a high emotion. Now that was an opportunity. In such moments as that, if the excitement is religious, wholesale conversions take place—tremendous temporary upliftments of the soul. I daresay those people afterwards wondered why they had been so shaken. It was exceedingly good for them, but it is rarely that such an opportunity comes.

We make a little current something like that on a small scale by our group meditation. We are perhaps only a score or so instead of many thousands, but in its way such a meeting is a real opportunity; if we could take better advantage of it we should make more rapid progress, we should feel ourselves more greatly helped.

It is a great assistance if in a group there are a few who are capable of rising to high levels. It is a great uplift that we should be for a few moments in the presence of thought on a higher plane. It is one of the advantages that we gain from our association, from " the assembling of ourselves together " for such work as this.

Collective meditation, such as some Lodges have at the public lectures for a mixed crowd, is frankly not of much use. It just keeps the audience quiet for a 'few moments, but it does little more, because the avarage man does not know how to think at all.

The unfolding of the higher consciousness is one of the possibilities which lie open to humanity at the stage which it has now reached. Therefore it is to a greater or less extent open to every one of us and it is well worth our while to make some attempt in that direction, for the addition to our usefulness which success would bring is almost incalculable. That the greatest caution must be exercised is true, for the pitfalls are many; nothing should be undertaken without the advice and supervision of a trained psychic. But the world needs helpers possessed of these powers, and it is among Theosophical students that we may reasonably expect to find them. It is hardly necessary to point out how advantageous to our work is the ability to communicate at will with the Angels and with the so-called dead, and the force and precision which definite experience of the higher life will give to our teaching. The knowledge gained is of the greatest comfort to him who acquires it, for it removes for ever from his life all doubt and all sorrow; yet man should strive for that transcendent wisdom not for his own sake, but that he may render himself more extensively serviceable to his fellow creatures, for that is the aim of all true and faithful brethren throughout the world.